EARLY AMERICAN DECORATION MADE EASY

WITH 18 FULL-SIZE PATTERNS FOR FURNITURE AND TRAYS

by

Edith Cramer

Drawings by the Author

DOVER PUBLICATIONS, INC.
NEW YORK

Published in Canada by General Publishing Company, Ltd., 30 Lesmill Road, Don Mills, Toronto, Ontario.
Published in the United Kingdom by Constable and Company, Ltd., 10 Orange Street, London WC2H 7EG.

This Dover edition, first published in 1985, is an unabridged and slightly corrected republication of the work first published by Charles T. Branford Company, Boston, Mass., in 1951, under the title *Handbook of Early American Decoration*.

Manufactured in the United States of America
Dover Publications, Inc., 31 East 2nd Street, Mineola, N.Y. 11501

Library of Congress Cataloging in Publication Data

Cramer, Edith, 1905–
   Early American decoration made easy.

   Previously published as: Handbook of early American decoration.
   Reprint. Originally published: Boston : C. Branford, 1951.
   1. Stencil work—United States.   2. Decoration and ornament, Early American.   I. Title.
NK8662.C73   1985   745.7′3   84-18863
ISBN 0-486-24776-7 (pbk.)

Foreword

Everything has to be imagined before it becomes a fact. For a very long time I have imagined a book: one that would be inspirational as well as helpful, one that would tell the "why's and wherefore's" and would present enough material to make it simple and easy for the painter to undertake immediately a project of early American decoration.

I have attempted to supply in this book a variety of authentic designs, applicable to Chippendale, Queen Anne, lace-edge, and coffin lid trays, Hitchcock chairs, pine chests, and other useful items. I have presented simple but beautiful trays and furniture, which are available on the market today in the form of reproductions. The projects in this practical book embody the fundamentals of good design and should help the decorator to enter wider fields in this particular type of decoration.

For the beginner, the first three chapters contain important *basic information* and should be read carefully. Each succeeding chapter describes more fully the different types and methods of decoration.

Appreciation and thanks are extended to those who have been helpful in assembling the material for this book: The National Museum of Wales, Cardiff, Wales; The Cooper Union Museum, New York, New York; The Society for the Preservation of New England Antiquities, Boston, Massachusetts; Mr. W. L. Crowell, teacher and authority on early decorated furniture and trays; Mr. Raymond Krape, authority on decorated Pennsylvania tin and furniture. My thanks go, also, to the many friends who have lent encouragement and aid in securing photographs and records of authentic old patterns.

The methods and materials presented here have been used and tested over a period of years by the author. Methods have been simplified as much as possible, and materials needed for this painting have been held to a minimum. May this book add to your pleasures of painting and restoring your own heirlooms. May it enlighten and add to your knowledge so that you will be inspired to create new designs to decorate your home.

EDITH CRAMER.

Sutton, Massachusetts

Table of Contents

Tole Tray

CHAPTER I

Notes on the History of Japanned Trays

The art of japanning was first practiced in Great Britain during the latter part of the seventeenth century. The appearance of oriental lacquer work stimulated this process of imitation. Early japanned articles were made of wood, as were the oriental lacquered screens, boxes and furniture, but these were not so durable. Metal was substituted as a base and, later, papier-mâché.

The metal tray was first developed in Pontypool, Wales. The early trays were decorated with simple geometric designs in several colors on a black background. Later decorations included flowers, foliage, fruits and exotic birds. Different hues and shades of bronzes were used. Designs and pictures were often made entirely of colored bronze powders. Gold leaf and gold powder, but never gold paint, were used on a sized surface. Flower painting was popular throughout the entire period of tray painting.

One method or pattern type often overlapped another and so we find several kinds of decoration used in one period. The better artists originated the designs which were then executed by copyists in large quantities for export trade. Small stenciled trays were sold as low as eight shillings a dozen.

Tortoise-shell backgrounds were characteristic of Pontypool trays, while those using a meandering line pattern known as "Stormont" were most frequently produced in Usk. Black, blue, dark brown and crimson were popular background colors. Decorated articles consisted of tea and trinket trays, waiters, cheese dishes, bread trays, teapots, coffee urns, candlesticks, snuffers, canisters and dressing boxes. Thousands of finished trays were exported yearly.

In America various types of trays and metal articles were made and decorated. Stenciling was found to be an easy way to produce large numbers at a popular price. These articles were frequently embellished with hand-painted sprays, lines, and even an occasional hand-painted flower or fruit. Stenciling may be described simply as a hand process of decoration which clearly and sharply defines a form applied through a cut-out pattern which may be duplicated repeatedly in an exact reproduction.

Stenciling was applied to walls, floors, furniture and accessories. The different uses varied in the technique of application and in the medium used. On walls, the stenciled border framed the windows, doors and fireplaces and followed near the edges of slanted ceilings. Borders were also used to designate panels and units where other designs of urns, flowers, pineapples, acorns, etc., were to decorate the centers. These designs were executed on colored backgrounds of water paint.

Floors were stenciled to imitate tile or mosaic. In this case a hard-wearing floor paint was used. Pumpkin yellow, yellow ochre, Indian red, gray and brown were popular colors. Marbled effects were made by using a feather to apply black and white graining on a gray background. Imitation of carpet was done by arranging a border around the edges and dividing the center into squares or diamonds. Stenciled designs were fitted into these spaces. A yellow ochre background with blue and black stenciled design or with black, white and Indian red made attractive color combinations.

Stencils on trays were much finer and more intricate. Fruits, flowers, birds, animals, houses, trees, boats and numerous other motifs were used on trays as well as on furniture. We have often found similar stencils on trays and furniture. In painting our reproductions today, we take liberties and use our imagination and ingenuity in applying the decoration which is in keeping with the shape, and also in proportion with our tray or furniture.

In many attics and storage places, there are chairs, chests, boxes and other articles to be found which are suitable for decoration. The most popular and easiest method of decoration is stenciling. Stencils were used on Hitchcock chairs and Boston rockers. Chairs were usually grained to imitate natural wood finishes, such as mahogany or rosewood. Fancy chairs of the Sheraton type were decorated with gold-leaf designs or with free-hand bronze painting. Color was often used for the background on fancy chairs and on some Windsor chairs. Soft old green, old yellow and Venetian red were popular colors.

Among the decorated chests there were the distinctive Pennsylvania dower chests. Background colors were numerous and figures of unicorns, birds, tulips, pomegranates, angels, horses, people and geometric patterns were used to embellish these chests. Often the name of the owner and a date were placed on the front of the chest.

Many small ornaments were also applied with various techniques on such things as the old bride's boxes, document and trinket boxes, and on glass panels in mirrors and clock doors. This glass painting employed still another technique of painting often called "reverse painting," a truly descriptive phrase, as this method of glass painting is done with an opposite approach to the one usually employed in painting a picture on canvas. The foreground parts are painted first, principally the small details. One paints from foreground to background and on the back side of the glass. This necessitates painting on the back but watching the front of the glass to make sure that

2

the paint stays within its boundaries. Many of these glass paintings were very crude, but on the finer clocks and gold-leaf mirrors they were beautifully executed. An original old glass painting adds value to a mirror or clock.

Hitchcock chairs were decorated with stencils on a grained black background. Boston rockers were also stenciled. Hand-painted designs of flowers and scrolls were used on entire bedroom sets of furniture. Similar painting was used on some caneback chairs and children's furniture. Grained backgrounds were made by applying black paint over a base of dry red paint, the graining being achieved by wiping away the wet black paint with a tool or crumpled cloth or paper, allowing the red to show through. Another graining effect was done by staining clean new wood with black striping or graining done with a brush. Later a brown varnish was painted over this black graining, giving the effect of brown wood, such as walnut.

Pennsylvania painted chairs were much brighter in color. Background colors were brighter and the designs were bolder. Pennsylvania furniture seems more closely related to the peasant furniture of Europe in color and design. Large cupboards, wall shelves and boxes were decorated with ornamental flowers and figures.

CHAPTER II

How to Restore Old Decorated Tinware

In restoring old decorated tinware, our first concern is to determine whether the design is a good one. Is it worth our while to restore it? We will have to admit that some of the early decorators were better artists than others; so let us choose a good design for restoration, one that is suitable for the tin on which it once was painted.

If there is no indication of the original pattern, then use one from a similar piece of tinware. If there is a pattern discernible, but very dim, clean the tin with mild soap and water, or clean carefully with denatured alcohol. Do this very cautiously until you can see the pattern. Trace around the pattern lines with your white conté pencil to make them more visible. Place a piece of frosted acetate (a cellophane-like material) over this and make a complete detailed tracing. Make notes on the colors, or even better, mix paints to match the colors and paint the design on the frosted acetate. *Copy every line, every detail.* This will be your record for your future work of an exact restoration. Note carefully the striping.

Clean the tin by applying paint remover (which can be bought at a paint store). Read the instructions on the can of paint remover and proceed as directed. Use an old paintbrush to apply the remover to the tin, as it is very hard on the hands. With the aid of a putty knife, excelsior or old cloths, wipe off the softened old paint. Have plenty of newspapers handy to catch all the messy paint and rags. Do this work out of doors if possible. Sandpaper should be used to remove the last bits of paint and to rough up the rusted and corroded places on the tin. Next apply rust remover with a cheap, dime store paintbrush. Rust remover may also be bought at a paint store. Again read the instructions on the container and follow them closely.

After all rust is removed, wash the tray thoroughly with scouring powder and a stiff brush, but do this quickly so the tin will not have a chance to start rusting again. Dry thoroughly with a clean cloth and wipe the tray with alcohol. Just before applying paint, wipe again with a tack cloth. A tack cloth is a cloth that has been treated to make it slightly tacky or sticky. It may be purchased from your art supply dealer. This gathers all the dust particles from the tray. It should be kept in a pint fruit jar

4

with a tight cover to keep it from drying out. Keep it stored in a cool place away from the sun.

The first coat of paint is metal primer or sanding primer. Sanding primer comes in gray or red and either one may be used on your tinware. Be sure to stir it well. If it seems too thick, it may be thinned a bit with turpentine. Do not use a coarse bristle brush. In all our work, we prefer softer brushes and thin paint. Apply the sanding primer evenly over the back or underside of the tray. Set this on nails that have been driven part of the way into a block of wood, then apply the primer to the top of the tray. Let it dry thoroughly (twenty-four hours).

Sandpaper the tray with waterproof sandpaper and water until it is smooth all over. This sandpaper is also known as wet-or-dry. Number 200 is fast, but use carefully and add just enough water to keep surface wet. This prevents the paint dust from clogging the surface of the sandpaper. Waterproof sandpaper is a special sandpaper that does not disintegrate in water, oil or fluids, like ordinary sandpaper. Give it another coat of sanding primer if any bare metal is exposed. Rub again with waterproof sandpaper until smooth.

Wash the tray and dry it thoroughly. Wipe off with a tack cloth. Mix drop black japan paint with turpentine until it is a little thinner than coffee cream. Japan paint comes in tubes or small, half-pint cans and has a thick paste consistency. It must be thinned before using. Add to your thinned japan paint about two teaspoons of varnish as this will help to give it a harder finish.

Use a soft, large camel-hair brush (1 inch to 1½ inches) to brush on the japan paint — first, on the bottom of the tray. Place it on the nails and then paint the top. Do not brush over your paint as the brush strokes will add more paint, causing it to pile up, and the surface will not be smooth.

Two thin coats, spaced twenty-four hours apart, are better than one heavy coat of paint. If japan paint is not thinned enough, it will have ridges caused by the bristles of the brush or by overlapping. It dries very rapidly, and therefore must be brushed on *quickly*. *Do not sand this black paint* — and do not attempt to save mixed japan paint for any length of time. It is better to mix only the amount required for one coat and mix a new batch when you are ready to apply a second coat. Be sure to wait twenty-four hours between coats of paint *always*.

After twenty-four hours, dust lightly with the tack cloth and varnish the tray with a quick-drying varnish. Use an ox-hair brush (1½ inch single). Pour about two tablespoons of varnish into a clean small dish (for a small tray, judge the amount according to the size of your tray). Dip your brush into the varnish and then spread it on the tray liberally, starting in the center and spreading the varnish toward the edges. We say to spread it liberally, but do not overdo it. It must not run in swoops on the rim, nor stand in puddles on the floor. Allow this varnish to dry for several days. Lightly buff the tray with 4/0 steel wool before transferring the pattern to the tray. The varnish will protect your background paint, and will permit erasures of mistakes made during the painting of the pattern. After the light rubbing with steel wool, the tray is ready for either stenciling, gold leaf or hand-painting.

Note: To prepare colored backgrounds, use colors in japan paint and prepare the same as the black japan paint was mixed. Apply three or more coats (twenty-four hours apart), until the sanding primer is completely covered. Proceed the same as in the preparation of black background. The color may be modified by adding other colors to soften the tone or to make it darker. To make it lighter add white enamel undercoat, which is a flat white paint.

Tints may be made of white enamel undercoat to which is added japan colors or tube oil colors, to reach the desired value. A tiny bit of black or raw umber may be added to soften the color.

How to Prepare Furniture for Decoration

In order to restore old furniture, we must first make a faithful record of the design which was on the article originally. Wash off the soil or film that has accumulated over the years. If soap and water do not clean it sufficiently, use clean cloths and alcohol to wipe away carefully the old shellac and dirt.

In some cases we have actually uncovered complete designs under a thick coat of old paint by using paint remover very carefully, wiping off with a cloth shortly after applying the remover so that it will not soften the paint too deeply. After the design has been uncovered, make a record on frosted acetate, by placing this material over the design and tracing it accurately, in every detail, with a pencil. Paint with color or bronzes on the frosted acetate to match the original design. Make a record also of striping and small details. Make a complete record before removing all paint from the furniture.

Have the furniture repaired and glued to make it firm again. In the case of chairs, have the seats renewed after the paint has been removed from the chairs — but before you start to repaint the chair.

Clean off the old paint either by scraping or by using paint remover. This is a messy job and is better done out of doors, for you need good

6

ventilation. Have plenty of rags and old newspapers ready. A wad of excelsior is good for getting the paint off the turnings of chairs. Wear plastic coated gloves to protect your hands. Apply the remover as directed on the container, wiping off the softened paint with rags, putty knife, newspapers or whatever works best for you. When you have removed all old paint, wash the chair with mineral spirits (substitute for turpentine). Allow the chair to dry thoroughly.

Sand with No. 00 sandpaper until all parts are smooth. Do not leave any particles of old paint, as the roughness will show through subsequent coats of paint. This will mar the appearance of the finished article. Apply a thin coat of orange shellac to act as a sealer.

Furniture may be painted in colors or it may be grained to imitate wood finishes. Old Hitchcock chairs and Boston rockers had grained finishes, black with bits of Venetian red showing through. This was done by painting the chair with Venetian red japan paint (this comes in paste form in tubes or in half-pint cans). Thin the japan paint with turpentine and add one or two teaspoons of varnish. About one-third cup is ample for a large chair, but the paint must be thin and spread evenly with a soft camel-hair brush.

Twenty-four hours later, mix black japan paint (thinned with turpentine — add varnish as in red paint mixture). Make this mixture very thin. Dip a bristle brush into the black paint, wipe out the brush on the edge of the dish and apply the remaining paint by dragging the brush over the surface on its heel. A wavering stroke makes a more interesting graining. Paint a small portion at one time, as the paint dries rapidly, but paint a complete side of a chest, or a complete panel of a chair, etc. We prefer to keep the main panel of a chair where the decoration appears, without graining. Paint it flat black.

An easier way to grain a chair is to apply the black paint over a portion of the chair (over the first red coat), such as the two front legs and cross piece. Then take a rag and wipe off the black paint in places to permit the red to show through, simulating a grained effect. Take your time and work out the graining as you go along. Do not rely on patching it later as patches tend to show.

Twenty-four hours later, varnish the grained chair or chest and set it aside to dry thoroughly. We always apply a protecting coat of varnish, for it allows us to erase mistakes when stenciling or painting. Striping is more successfully done on a varnished surface.

Some pieces of furniture and some chairs and boxes require coats of paint in color. Favorite colors were Venetian red, old yellow, olive green, old blue, soft gray green and dark brown. To make the lighter colors, we use enamel undercoat which is a flat white. We tint it with oil colors in tubes to the desired color. Practically all colors may be grayed by adding a bit of black, or raw umber. Several thin coats of paint will give a better and smoother surface than a thick one. The color will appear lighter when it is dry, but will regain its depth when varnished.

The darker colors should be bought in flat finish paint, already mixed, as near the shade we want as we can find. We may have to modify the color by adding other colors from tubes of oil paint. It is advisable to stir the paint for a very *long* time, as it takes much longer than we think to mix the paint thoroughly. Strain the paint through double thickness of an old nylon stocking. *Always* strain colored paints before applying to the furniture. After the first coat, cover the paint tightly to save it for future coats. Before the second coat, stir it well and strain it again before using. Strain it before the third coat.

Before beginning the decoration on the furniture, cover the last coat of colored paint with varnish and let it dry for forty-eight hours or more. You might save some of the background color to use for patching in case of need.

8 *Examples of Free-Hand Brush Strokes*

CHAPTER III

Stenciling

Stenciling was a method used to decorate trays, chairs, boxes and other articles with greater speed. With the addition of a few washes of transparent color, sprays of leaves, fine lines or curlicues, a very decorative pattern could be achieved. The stencils used by the early decorators were usually cut from paper and hence very fragile. For our stencils, we find that architect's linen is to be preferred as it is thin and strong and will stand wear.

To make stencils, place the linen, dull side up, over the tracing of the design. Since the linen is semi-transparent, the design will be visible so that you may trace it with a pencil on the linen. Be sure to provide enough linen to make a margin of one inch around all sides of the motif which is to be cut out. Most designs are composed of many parts. In a bowl of fruit, each piece of fruit is cut on a separate stencil and the bowl on still another.

Stencil Traced on Linen

Stencil After Cutting,
Placed Over Black Background

Stencil patterns given in this book are ready for transfer on most popular size trays. They are actual patterns taken from the author's repertoire.

Use a pair of sharp pointed embroidery or manicure scissors to cut out the fruit. It is the linen margin around the fruit which becomes our stencil, so cut carefully and do not stretch the edges as you cut. This procedure is carried out with each fruit, leaf, bowl or other part of the pattern. For small round holes, we suggest using a large darning needle. Punch through the linen carefully. Use No. 600 sandpaper to sand the rough edges on the underside. Repeat several times until the hole appears neat and round.

When cutting a flower or spray where many openings have to be cut, always start with the smallest ones first so as to prevent weakening of the stencil while working on it. Care should be taken to prevent wrinkles. Stencils should be kept pressed between the pages of a book in order to keep them perfectly flat.

When you first buy your architect's linen, take it home, unroll it, cut it up in pieces not exceeding fifteen inches in size and keep it pressed flat between the back leaves of your tracing paper pad. When you are ready to make stencils, the linen will be flat and easy to handle.

Have a tracing of your pattern before you as you work in order to check the arrangement of the different stencil parts. A key stencil may be made by tracing on a piece of linen large enough to cover the entire pattern, a portion of a leaf, fruit or bowl, to provide a guide for each separate unit as you stencil. If the complete pattern is to be placed several times on a tray or a set of chairs, the key stencil is necessary in order that the patterns may all be in the same proportion and arrangement.

Suppose you are stenciling a tray. First, the tray must be smooth as glass. We assume that you have already used the metal primer and two coats of black paint, and a coat of varnish. To make the tray smooth, use black waterproof sandpaper No. 600 with water to rub the tray thoroughly until it feels absolutely smooth to your fingertips. Any little roughness, or ridge from the bristles of the paintbrush, will show through the gold stenciling. After the tray is smooth, rinse off with water and dry thoroughly.

Have your stencils and your tracing arranged near your table. Place the tray on the table at a comfortable working height. Wipe off dust with a tack cloth. Varnish the portion that is to be stenciled with regular slow-drying varnish, brushing out very thin. While waiting for this to become nearly dry, prepare your bronze powder palette.

This palette is made by fitting a piece of cotton velvet in a shallow box about nine by twelve inches. Place bits of bronze powders on this velvet about two inches apart, starting with silver, lemon gold, xx gold, deep gold, copper, fire, and matt green. These colors will be sufficient for most of your needs. Have several small pieces of velvet three inches square. Hem the edges or use nail polish on the edges to prevent raveling.

Test the tray by touching it lightly with your fingertip to determine when it is nearly dry. It should be so nearly dry that no mark of your finger will show on the varnish. However, it should have a feeling of clinging to your finger. This sticky stage is referred to as "tacky." At the tacky stage we are ready to start stenciling.

10

In this book we have given a design for a tray which is a combination of stenciling, gold leaf, and some hand-painting. The stenciled portion is on the floor of the tray. This is done *after* the gold-leaf band is applied. Directions for the band have been given elsewhere.

Our first problem was to decide the number of times the flower group was to be repeated. We have used it twice on the long side of the tray, and once on the end.

Place the center flower of the group in these six places, twice on each side and once on the ends. Wrap the index finger with a small piece of velvet and secure with a rubber band, just tightly enough to keep the velvet from falling off. Dip this finger lightly into the desired color of bronze powder (usually the lightest), and work it into the velvet by rubbing it against the back of your left hand or on a pad of cloth. Too much powder will spoil your first attempt, so use it sparingly for you may always go back for more. Place this finger with gold powder on the linen and work over to the edges of the cutout flower.

Use a circular motion to cover all the tips of the petals. To make some areas appear shadowed, apply less gold, allowing more of the black background to show through. This flower should be left dark in the center. There should be no excess gold powder on the linen if you have used just the amount necessary to make the flower. Lift the linen stencil carefully. Stencil each of the central flowers in the same way in their designated places on the tray.

Place the second flower unit to one side of the flower you have just stenciled. Rub in the second shade of powder (which will be the next deeper shade of gold). Repeat this flower unit on the other side of the central flower. Stencil in the same manner on all of the groupings on the tray.

Place the large leaves at the ends of each group and stencil in deeper gold or copper. These leaves are made to fade into shadow near the flowers by using less powder. The tiny spray stencil is used to fill in empty areas to make the border more clearly defined.

If this is your first attempt at stenciling, try out the design and get some practice by using a piece of black oilcloth instead of your tray. Varnish the oilcloth, and when it is tacky, stencil it as we have directed. By experiment, you will discover how much bronze powder to use and how to apply it.

If your tray dried before you could finish your stenciling, set it aside until the next day. *Do not* attempt to wipe off any excess powder. The next day, wash your tray thoroughly with water and dry it with a soft cloth. This is to remove all loose bronze powder. Wipe off lightly with a tack cloth and apply another coat of varnish over the floor of the tray. Set it aside until it is tacky, and then resume stenciling where you left off the day before. Apply any details that were omitted the previous day, such as the center detail of the center flower. Then allow the tray to dry for at least forty-eight hours. Wash off the loose gold bronze particles. Use the black background paint to obliterate smudges, or mistakes. Clean up rough edges by painting around them with this same black paint.

At this stage, striping may be done. Use a mixture of gold powder and varnish and a small striping quill. Place a small stripe on the floor three-eighths of an inch from the bend of the tray and another one-quarter inch from the edge of the rim.

Clean the stencils by laying them flat on a clean paper and wiping them carefully with a clean cloth moistened with cleaning fluid or carbon tetrachloride. All varnish and powder must be removed from both sides of the stencils. Allow them to dry well and then place them between the pages of a book until needed again.

Use India ink to number the stencil parts to correspond with the numbers on the pattern. This makes it easier to find the parts quickly when we are stenciling.

Gold Leaf

Gold leaf never loses its luster, and therefore is much desired for decoration on the fine trays, boxes, and other articles. It was used for elaborate scroll borders on Chippendale or scalloped trays and for double borders on the better coffin lid trays. Occasionally we find a small unit of gold leaf on a stenciled tray. A combination of stenciled units and gold leaf has been used on many fine pieces of furniture during the early part of the nineteenth century.

Gold leaf should be applied over an oil size to obtain the best results. This requires a waiting period from twelve to twenty-four hours between the time the size was applied until the time the gold leaf must be laid.

To accelerate this process, varnish is substituted for the oil size. For class work, we recommend the varnish size, but for those who do this work at home, we recommend oil size to give a smoother and more beautiful luster to the finished product.

Have your tray prepared as directed in Chapter II. Rub down the protecting coat of varnish with waterproof black sandpaper No. 600 and water until it is absolutely smooth. Rinse off and dry thoroughly. *Do not use a tack cloth to dust your tray.* This is one time we refrain from using

12

the tack cloth. Sprinkle the tray with talcum powder and wipe off with a soft dry clean cloth. Keep your fingers off the tray as much as possible for gold leaf will adhere to the slightest moisture or stickiness.

Transfer your pattern to the tray by using lithopone-prepared paper. *Never use a wax tracing paper.*

Prepare your own tracing paper by rubbing lithopone powder on a piece of paper taken from your tracing pad. Rub one side of the paper with lithopone powder, applied with a wad of cotton. Rub into the paper with your bare fingers. Fold paper so that the powdered surface is inside. Keep it stored in your tracing pad for future use.

After your tracing is completed on your tray, use a sable brush to paint your pattern, using varnish as your gold size. Start at one point on the tray and proceed in one direction, painting in all parts as you go. Paint the large units first, and small details and lines next. You may need to change from a large to a small brush. Apply size from the center of this area toward the edges, to prevent thick or ridgy edges. Do not skip around on your pattern but paint all parts as you proceed around your tray. After you have painted four or five inches, test the first part painted to determine the tackiness. Touch it with a clean fingertip. It must be nearly dry, for after gold leaf is applied, it excludes the air from the size, causing it to dry very slowly. If the gold is applied when the size is too wet, the gold leaf will wrinkle and may be disturbed or lifted with subsequent coats of varnish.

To mount loose gold leaf, open the little book very carefully until a sheet of gold is exposed. Place a piece of wax paper, a little larger than the gold, on top of the sheet of gold. Place your hand on top of the wax paper. The warmth of your hand will cause the gold to adhere to the wax paper. Lift the paper and cut in two with a pair of sharp scissors. It is easier to handle it in smaller pieces. The extra margin of wax paper is necessary in order to handle the gold as you must not touch the gold with your fingers. Gold leaf comes in mounted form also and is labeled "for gilding in the wind." Either kind may be used in our decorative work.

When the varnished area on the tray is tacky (almost dry), lay a portion of the mounted gold leaf on top, with the gold side down. With a small soft wad of cotton, gently rub over the wax paper. The gold should leave the wax paper and adhere to the varnish when you lift the paper. Do not worry about the ragged bits of loose gold. Continue to lay the gold only up to the point where the varnished area is at the proper tacky stage. Stop and resume painting in the pattern with the gold size for another four or five inches, and then test again where you left off applying gold leaf to see when you may apply more gold leaf and how far you may apply it. Continue until you have covered the entire pattern. Take a soft piece of cotton and brush off the excess gold leaf, brushing very lightly as it is very easy to mar the gold.

If there is very much etching to be done on your pattern, we suggest that you do not attempt to lay more gold than you will have time to etch. Etching should be done the *same day* the gold leaf is laid. If etching is attempted after the gold is hard dry, there is a chance that the gold will come off in chips, making a ragged line. For a single etcher we use an 8H pencil sharpened to a fine point. Should you desire a heavier line, the point can be made blunt by rubbing the pencil point on fine sandpaper. Etchers of more than one point may be purchased from your art supply store.

In etching leaves, start with a single etcher to draw in the main veins. Use a double etcher to draw in the fine lines on the shadow sides, which will be near the base of the leaf, along one side of the main veins and pos-sibly on the lower outer edges of the leaf. Fruits and flowers are etched along the shadow sections. The lines should conform to the shape of the leaf or fruit. After the gold is hard dry (several days), it is then given a coat of varnish. After the tray is dry, the etched portions are shaded with burnt umber or brown pink.

On elaborate trays, where birds have been laid in gold or palladium leaf (palladium leaf has the appearance of silver), color glazes are used of alizarin crimson or Prussian blue. Prussian blue over gold becomes green. If you wish it to remain blue use palladium leaf instead of gold under Prussian blue.

The Chippendale design given in Chapter VII, decorated with gold leaf and mother-of-pearl, came from an authentic old tray. Transparent color was used for a glaze over parts of the pearl and on the flowers. Gold leaf was also used to make the band on the rectangular tray in Chapter V. Large Chippendale trays seem to require gold leaf for their elaborate bor-ders. The shape of the tray suggests to us a handsome border and an elaborate center pattern.

To make fine lines in gold for curlicues and other feathery line work, use a fine pen and a mixture of varnish and fine gold powder. Mix the varnish and powder in a bottle cap to the depth of less than a quarter inch. Do not overload the pen point. Pen lines should be made on a varnished surface. Frequent cleaning of the pen point is necessary. Gold leaf may be applied to the fine lines if desired. Allow the tray to dry thoroughly before removing the excess gold.

Mother-of-pearl was used principally on papier-maché furniture, trays, boxes, and cabinets. However, it has been found on many metal trays. Since mother-of-pearl is not always available, we suggest as a substitute

14

that palladium leaf be used on the areas designated for mother-of-pearl. Apply varnish medium or gold size on these areas, and when almost dry cover them with palladium leaf. After this is dry (several days later) brush off the loose palladium leaf and cover the areas with varnish medium. Blend into this wet varnish a bit of alizarin crimson and a bit of Prussian blue, making a variegated effect to the color blending. This makes a very satisfactory imitation of mother-of-pearl.

While the mother-of-pearl is drying the gold-leaf work may be done, provided you cover the pearl parts with paper secured with masking tape. After the gold-leaf work is completely dry, the entire tray should be varnished in order to protect the gold while further painting and glazes are applied. This coat of varnish should dry for several days.

A glaze is made by mixing a small amount of transparent color with varnish. This is applied quickly and evenly over the area planned for it. Do not work in it too long with your brush or it will begin to dry and will not be smooth. The more sure your brush stroke is, the better the result. Some of the transparent colors are alizarin crimson, rose madder, terre verte, viridian, Indian yellow, gamboge, brown pink, Prussian blue, burnt umber, ivory black and the lake colors.

Glazes were also used over mother-of-pearl. Details were made on pearl with India ink and pen before the glaze was applied. The glazes are applied only on the shadow sides, leaving the natural pearl for the lights.

When finishing a tray on which mother-of-pearl has been used, it is necessary to use more than the usual six coats of varnish, in order to build up the background to the thickness of the pearl. Apply additional coats of varnish, rubbing lightly with steel wool 4/0 between coats, until the surface has been built up to the desired smoothness. More coats of thin varnish will be needed than of a heavier varnish. However, the heavier varnish requires longer drying time. *Twenty-four hours is a minimum drying time for any paint or varnish*, but it is better to wait four days or more for varnish to dry before applying more varnish. *Be sure to allow each coat ample time to dry thoroughly.* For complete instructions on finishing trays refer to Chapter XI.

Painting in Color

In the painting of country tin we have learned the necessity of perfect brush stroke. Perfect brush stroke is a requisite in all painting. When we have mastered this technique, we will find that a few strokes can form a flower petal or a leaf and, at the same time, can blend the colors into a pleasing arrangement of light and shade. Quill brushes are excellent for blending and for making soft fragile flowers.

On some of the old trays the flower painting was done by applying glazes of transparent colors over a foundation or underpainting of flat white and black. This underpainting was a contour painting of lights and shadows, using the white on the lightest part of the flower and then adding black to make varying shades of gray which modeled the form of the flower into its deepest shadows. Much time was spent by early decorators on the underpainting as it had to be as nearly perfect as possible. After this painting was dry, glazes of transparent color and varnish were applied very thinly over the light areas and heavier glazes over the dark areas. After the glaze was dry, additional glazes of other colors were added for a variation in tone. Final touches were painted with white in order to accent the edges of petals. The same method was used on the leaves.

We prefer to use a bit of local color when painting an underpainting for flowers and leaves, for we find the finished product has a deeper and richer color. For instance, in painting a yellow rose, add a bit of yellow ochre to the white for the middle tones. White is used for the lightest part of the rose. In the deep center and under the cup of the rose add ochre and burnt sienna, omitting white entirely. This foundation should be a blended mass of color, with no petals outlined. It is accomplished by patting the area lightly with your finger or a dry brush. Do not draw or designate the petals in any way.

First Shading of Foundation, Step 1   *Petals Drawn with Fine White Lines, Step 2*

Painting a Rose

After this foundation is thoroughly dry, a bit of raw sienna and white in varnish is used as a glaze over the light portions. This glaze should be very transparent and extended slightly beyond the outline of the rose, giving the edges a "filmy" appearance. This makes the rose seem more transparent and fragile. A few hairlines of white are used to draw in the petals.

16

This same method may be used on other flowers. Do not extend the filmy white paint on shadow sides of the flowers.

Green leaves are first painted with a middle tone of green, softened with raw umber. This color should be a soft green, slightly grayed. After it is dry, glaze the shadows with a darker green, which may be viridian with burnt umber. If this seems too brown, add Prussian blue to offset the brownish tones. All leaves should be darkened near flowers. Shadows usually follow the main vein at the base of the leaves and diminish toward the middle area, leaving the tips light.

The light areas of leaves are made of a lighter tone of the first green used. Add to this a bit of chrome yellow light. The final touches are the light veins and accents. Make a very light green by adding white to your lightest green, also a bit of raw umber to soften it. With a fine quill brush, accent the upper edges of the leaves with fine white lines (broken at places). Do not carry the lines into the shadows, accent only the light parts. Draw the veins in this same light color. Careful accents and lights will add beauty to your flowers.

To make the dark side of the leaf fade into the background, take a bit of black and pat it on the shadow side of the leaf with your finger, making the edge of the leaf appear very dim.

Most curlicues and tendrils around flower groupings are painted with a lighter tone than the leaves, but are darkened where they disappear behind the leaves. These tendrils should be very thin and delicate.

To paint a wild rose, first smudge the center with light olive green. Mix some white with raw umber to obtain a soft white. As we paint the petals with our first coat, we draw the brush with one long stroke from tip of petal to the center. Paint all petals this way and then gently pat the entire flower to make a smooth surface, obliterating all brush marks. The flower should have a shadow center and the edges of the petals should be very thin. Never let the paint build up thick edges to your petals. Allow this basic coat to dry thoroughly.

A glaze of alizarin crimson and varnish is applied to the shadow sides of the petals and a bit of alizarin crimson is patted on the center. On this dark center place a few dots of soft yellow made by adding white and burnt umber to chrome yellow medium. Make stamens radiating from the center, with darker yellow dots on the ends of the stamens. Accent the light edges of the petals with a thin line of white and darken a few shadow edges with a glaze of alizarin crimson and burnt umber (in varnish).

Small sprays of flowers and leaves help to make a bouquet lacy and graceful. Fuchsias, bleeding hearts, lilies of the valley, forget-me-nots, and tiny bell-shaped flowers should be painted carefully. Most of these require

17

an underpainting in a tone slightly darker than the finished flower. Most white flowers should be painted in "off white" made by adding raw umber to white. After this first painting is dry, a glaze is used to darken the shadow side and a highlight of white on the light side. Shadows may have a slight greenish tinge, or a bit of blue or low-toned red.

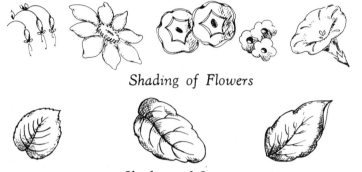

Shading of Flowers

Shading of Leaves

The underpainting of red flowers such as fuchsias and bleeding hearts should be made of Venetian red and white. The glaze should be made of alizarin crimson or crimson lake. Use black to darken alizarin crimson.

Free-Hand Bronze Painting

Free-hand bronze painting differs from regular painting in the fact that we use colored bronzes instead of oil paints. The pattern is painted with black varnish medium, and allowed to dry to the tacky stage. Colored bronzes are carefully brushed into the edges and light areas with a dry brush. The bronze powders are not mixed with a medium but are applied *dry* with a *dry brush*, brushing carefully from the background into the edges of the flower or leaf. This will appear to smudge the background, but if your background paint was thoroughly dry, the powder will wash off the background easily after your pattern has dried. Do *not* attempt to wash it while the pattern is wet as the bronzes must stay on the varnished pattern. Flowers may be painted in this way with several shades of gold and silver but only one overlapping petal or leaf may be done at one time. For instance, a silver flower and green leaf which touch each other may not be painted at the same time, as the silver powder may spread over to the leaf and the green powder may settle on the silver flower. Shading of the bronzes may be accomplished by using very little powder in the shadow areas, but applying the powder very thickly on the *lighter* areas and edges.

Veins are drawn either with India ink or painted with gold bronze powder and varnish. Fine line tendrils may be added with a fine brush and bronze powder mixed with varnish.

18

CHAPTER IV

Document Box

In the field of early decorated tin, we find boxes of all shapes and sizes used as receptacles to store valuable papers, trinkets, money, souvenirs and other things too numerous to mention. Some tin was shaped like chests, trunks, canisters, round boxes, oval boxes, and others came in fancy shapes, including an adaptation of the Chippendale tray shape. They were painted in colors as well as sober black and were embellished with flowers, fruits, birds, landscapes and a more primitive type of decoration simplified to brush stroke design.

The design shown here was found on an old trunk-shaped box which measured four and one-half inches high and eight and one-half inches wide on the front surface where the principal decoration was executed. It was beautifully painted with excellent brush strokes used in the development of the flowers and leaves.

The background of the original box was asphaltum. This is a dark brown, semi-transparent varnish surface and does not wear very well as it scratches and chips easily. Instead, we suggest the use of a flat black or brown paint for the ground color. Trace the design on your box, using lithopone tracing paper. Paint the leaves and stems in dark olive green made with Prussian blue, raw umber and yellow. For our darker greens use chrome yellow medium (where yellow is mixed with blue to make green), and for the lighter greens use chrome yellow light in mixing greens. These leaves (see page 20) should be painted with long strokes of the brush. A fairly large brush is necessary, either a No. 3 or 4 sable brush. Varnish medium should be mixed with the paints. If it becomes too thick and sticky to enable you to make good brush strokes, thin your paint with a small amount of turpentine, but use the turpentine sparingly. Sometimes it is better to mix a fresh batch of paint. After all the leaves are painted with the dark green, mix some lighter green and add a few light strokes on the upper side of the leaves.

Paint the two center flowers in Venetian red, also the two oval fruits. Do *not* paint the small sprays that grow from the centers of these flowers. Paint the two end flowers with old white (white and raw umber), using long, sure strokes from the tips of the petals to the base of the center vein.

19

Figure 1.

Trunk
Document Box

A RED
B WHITE
C YELLOW
D GREEN

Use the same white to paint the spray of leaves growing from the center of the red flower on the left. The spray of the other red flower is painted in yellow. Allow the painting to *dry* before adding details.

Yellow strokes are painted in the centers of the white flowers radiating from the base into a fan-shaped pattern. Yellow details in the flower centers are added to the red flowers as shown by the pattern. Add white highlights to the petals and red fruits. Add radiating red lines to the white flower centers. Mix old yellow, using chrome yellow medium, raw umber and yellow ochre to paint the border along the front of the lid and to stripe the front, the ends and the top of the trunk. Decorate around the handle on top with a few well-defined brush strokes. These should be made with one sweep of the brush.

Document or Trinket Box

All accessory pieces of tinware that are not subject to hard usage may be finished with two coats of spar varnish and one coat of "rubbed effect," or satin finish varnish. We recommend waxing with a paste wax for a final finish, as it helps to prevent scratches.

Bread Tray

Many of the old painted tinware pieces were very useful as well as decorative and among these we find tea caddies, boxes, candle holders, food warmers, egg cookers, tin flasks, teapots and coffee urns, candle boxes, tin canisters of all shapes, match holders, and an array of other wares.

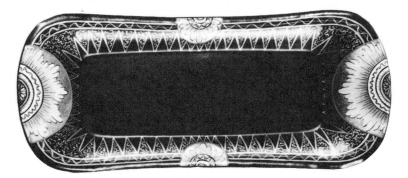

Snuffer Tray

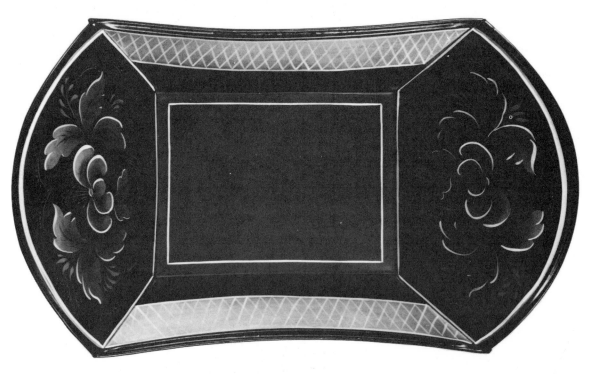

Bread Tray

Photograph 1

22

23

Figure 2.   Corner of Bread Tray

Center of Star Flower

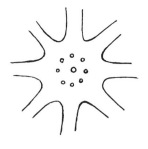

Handle

Figure 3. Design for Bellows

The original bread tray from which this design was taken had a soft blue-green background. The ends of this tray are shaped similarly to the apple dishes with sloping sides. The design is free-hand painting with brushed-on gold and silver highlights on the leaves and flowers. Other dark background colors such as maroon, brown or black would look well on this tray. See Photograph No. 1.

Mark the bands one inch wide along the sides of the tray, using your white conté pencil. Plan to leave a margin all around the top edge of the tray, a quarter of an inch wide. Use black varnish medium to paint the bands. When tacky, apply silver powder to cover the band. Let this dry thoroughly, at least twenty-four hours. Wash off the excess silver powder with cold water and dry the tray with a soft cloth.

Mix old white (white and raw umber) for striping. We like an enamel *undercoat* for striping as it makes an opaque stripe. Scoop up some of the thickened pigment that has settled in the bottom of the can, mix with a bit of raw umber and thin to the proper consistency for striping, using turpentine and a bit of varnish medium. Remember that varnish medium has a tendency to make your white more transparent, so use only enough to keep the stripe from spreading and feathering. Place a stripe around the silver band. Continue the top stripe across the end panels. Stripe along the sides and bottom of the end panels. Use silver powder and varnish medium to stripe around the floor one-quarter inch from the edge. Use a small quill brush to draw the lattice work in white on the silver bands.

When this paint is dry (after twenty-four hours), trace the pattern on the end panels. Paint the flowers and large leaves with black varnish medium, using a No. 3 sable brush. When this reaches the tacky stage, brush silver powder on the flowers, leaving shadows at the center of the flower. Brush deep gold on the leaves.

Mix soft green (Prussian blue, raw umber, chrome yellow medium, and white) to paint the remainder of the small leaf sprays and stamens. Mark the veins in the large leaves with black paint. Top the stamens with yellow dots. Finish the tray with six coats of varnish. Rub down with pumice stone and oil. Refer to Chapter XI for directions on finishing.

Fireside Bellows

There are many shapes and sizes of fireside bellows to be found in antique shops. It is also possible to obtain new reproductions of this very practical and useful fireside implement. Designs vary from the simple stenciled ones found on flat-top bellows to the more elaborate hand-painted ones found on the turtle-back type. It is also true that simple designs were used on turtle-back bellows. The turtle-back bellows has a rounded top surface, its shape suggesting its name. The bellows pictured here is painted in old yellow and smoked over a candle to give it a clouded or marbleized background.

Antique Fireplace Bellows

If your bellows is an antique, have it repaired, including the leather. If the painting is done first, there is a chance that it will get scratched when the repair job is done, so repair first and paint last.

Tie a string to the nozzle so that it may be hung up to dry after your background paint has been applied.

The bellows shown above was given two thin coats of flat yellow made by mixing chrome yellow medium, yellow ochre and raw umber to white enamel *undercoat*. These two coats must be applied twenty-four hours apart. Immediately after the second coat, hold the bellows by the nozzle over a lighted candle (let the wick of the candle remain long so as to cause it to smoke, or place a nail across the top of the candle, causing an uneven flame). Move the bellows in various directions so that the smoke settles in swirls in the wet paint. Be careful to hold it far enough from the heat of the flame so that the paint will not blister. After it has been smoked to a nice pattern, hang it up to dry twenty-four hours.

On the following day, cover the bellows with a coat of varnish to protect the smoke finish. After the varnish is dry, rub the surface lightly

26

with fine steel wool. The pattern will take more clearly on a surface that has some "tooth" to it.

Trace the pattern (see page 24) on the bellows. Cut three stencils of architect's linen, the pear blossom end, the flower center, and the border motif. With a No. 3 sable brush and black varnish medium, paint in the star flowers, fruit and black band along the edge. When this black paint reaches the tacky stage, use a velvet-covered finger to apply the gold powder through the stencils to make the centers of the star flowers. Make the center bright, fading toward the edges. Remove the stencil and brush gold on the petal tips. Stencil the blossom end on the pear. Remove the stencil and smudge a large, round highlight on the body of the pear and a smaller one on the neck of the pear. Use the third stencil to apply the border design on the band around the edge.

Use black varnish medium to make the brush strokes as designated in the pattern around the fruits and flowers. Paint the large leaves in blue-green with black veins. (Make blue-green of Prussian blue, yellow, raw umber and white.) Other brush strokes around the flowers and fruits are painted in vermilion, as well as the small stripe that edges the inside of the black band, and the stripes on the handle. A few brush strokes in vermilion decorate the handle. The stamens of the flowers are painted in black.

After twenty-four hours, give the bellows a coat of varnish. After twenty-four hours apply a second coat to which a bit of burnt umber has been added for antiquing. Apply three more coats of varnish twenty-four hours apart. Finish by rubbing with pumice and oil as directed in Chapter XI.

Examples of Free-Hand Brush Strokes

Photograph 2. *Rectangular Tray*

CHAPTER V

Rectangular Tray with Rounded Corners

The rectangular tray with rounded corners was popular over a long period of time. It was adaptable to many different types of design, from the fine gold-leaf borders with much intricate detail, hand-painted trays with flowers, fruits, foliage and birds to the later ones decorated with stencils. We find some with center and border designs and others with border designs only.

One very beautiful tray of this type had a Persian landscape with figures and horses covering the entire floor of the tray. The rim was decorated with a fine conventionalized border of gold leaf and small painted detail in color, also Persian in feeling. Another very lovely tray had a border on the rim of gold-stenciled units which were outlined with white. Small gold ink lines in "Stormont" pattern (Pontypool design) filled the space between this border and a small gold stripe on the floor of the tray. The center of the tray was decorated with a small landscape, about six by eight inches in size, painted in color. Around this was painted another border in white and more pen and ink lines to harmonize with the border on the rim of the tray.

The design given on page 30 is for a tray eighteen by twenty-five inches. It can be used on a larger tray by adding or repeating the units of the design. However, it should not be used on a smaller tray as it would be too heavy. Have your tray prepared according to the General Instructions in Chapter II. As stated there, a protective coat of varnish must be applied to protect the final coat of black paint. This must be thoroughly dry or you will run into trouble when using gold leaf. You must also be sure to have your tray very smooth. This can be accomplished by using waterproof black sandpaper No. 600 and water. Rub lightly until the entire tray feels smooth to the fingertips. Rinse with water and dry carefully. Dust with talcum powder (this helps to prevent the gold leaf from adhering to the background where it is not wanted). Wipe off with a soft dry cloth.

The band on the rim may be made of gold-bronze powder or gold leaf. Draw the outline with your conté chalk pencil for the band one-fourth inch from the edge of the tray, making the band two inches wide. With a

Figure 4. Pattern for Tray with Rounded Corners

A FLOWER
B LEAF
C CENTER FLOWER
D LEAF

E FLOWER
F SILHOUETTE
G CENTER
H SPRAY

large flat sable brush and varnish medium or gold size, paint in this band in a thin even manner. When it is nearly dry or "tacky" the gold-bronze powder may be dusted on. A velvet pounce may be made by wrapping a large ball of cotton with velvet. Dip ball into the gold powder and brush lightly over the tacky varnish medium. Set aside to dry for forty-eight hours.

Gold leaf may be purchased by the book in either mounted or unmounted form. The mounted type is easier to use as each little sheet of gold is mounted on a small piece of tissue paper for easy handling and placement. You may even cut the sheet into smaller pieces with sharp scissors. Lift one of these small squares and place it on the tacky band of the tray — *gold leaf side down.* Press lightly with a small wad of cotton on every part of the gold. This will cause the gold to stick to the tacky surface. Now you can lift the small tissue paper and place the remaining gold on the next part of the sticky band. Continue this operation until you have covered the entire band on the tray. Lap the joints only enough to make sure that you have left no gaps. Several hours later you may lightly brush away the excess gold leaf with a soft piece of cotton. Use a *very light touch* as the gold mars easily while still wet. Permit the gold band to dry for a week. A word of precaution: do not attempt to do gold-leaf work on a rainy day, as it will not dry. While you are waiting for the gold-leaf band to become hard and dry, prepare the stencils for the floor of the tray and also the three stencil units for the rim.

For stencils, we recommend purchasing architect's linen from your art supply store. It is more durable than paper stencils — and may be used over and over again. A very small pair of embroidery scissors or manicure scissors with sharp points is an excellent tool for cutting. Some people may prefer to use a stencil knife.

Place the linen, dull side up (it is semi-transparent), over the pattern and trace on to the linen the outline of the flower or leaf. Leave a margin of an inch around all sides of the leaf or flower. This tracing may be made with pencil or pen. With a coarse needle, pierce the center of the leaf or flower. This helps the tiny scissors to get started in cutting out the leaf. Discard the leaf and keep the remaining part which is your stencil. All edges must be smooth and clean-cut and must not be stretched. If the edges should happen to be stretched, the gold powder will creep under when we use the stencil and it will result in a fuzzy and messy design. While cutting, always turn your stencil in such a position as to relieve strain on the stencil. Otherwise, it will stretch. You may turn your stencil in any direction in order to favor cutting — even cut from the reverse side as the pattern is visible from either side. Always cut tiny dots and lines *first.* Cutting

31

large parts will weaken the stencil and make it difficult to cut smaller parts. Prepare each of the units carefully and number according to the diagram, using drawing ink. Other markings will be erased when you clean your stencils, so it is necessary to use India ink or drawing ink for this purpose.

After the gold leaf has dried for a week or more, prepare to do the stenciling in a dust-free room. Wipe the tray with a wet cloth, being careful to wipe the edges, as little particles of gold leaf and dust have a way of hanging on just over the edges, and may be picked up with your varnish brush at the wrong time. Dry with a soft cloth. Wipe with a tack cloth before varnishing.

Dip your varnish brush into the slow-drying varnish and cover the entire tray, beginning in the center and working up over the rim. Be sure you have applied a thin even coat, leaving no puddles. It is important to have the varnish evenly distributed, not too skimpily and not too lavishly. The right amount you will learn with practice. Too much varnish causes uneven drying, too little varnish does not give depth to your stenciling. Set aside to dry to the tacky stage. After thirty minutes, touch it lightly with your fingertip. If it sticks very much, it is not ready. Test at intervals until it reaches the stage when it adheres only very slightly and leaves no mark of your finger.

Stencil No. 1 is placed three times along each side of the tray and also three times across the end, and yet the spaces between are even. Notice that the three end stencils reach the corners. The flower stencils along the side do not come close to the corners of the tray. The end flowers take care of the space at the corners.

Note carefully the placing before you begin to stencil as you will not be able to make any erasures. A simple way to start is to place the flower (unit No. A) in the exact center of the end of the tray *on the gold band*. (Have your palette of bronze powders ready as you will need several colors for this design.) When you have your flower No. A in place, use a velvet-wrapped finger to apply silver powder over the entire flower. Repeat this at the other end of the tray. Then place the stencil in the exact center of the side of the tray *on the gold band*. Stencil with silver powder as before. Repeat on the other side. Apply only enough powder to fill in the pattern, leaving no excess on the linen.

Between these flowers you must judge your space, in order to apply the flower twice. It must be evenly spaced — so use care. This work should be done completely around the tray. After all flowers are placed, apply stencil No. B, the leaf, between the flowers. The angle of the leaf must be exactly the same each time, easing it around the corners. The leaf should be done in silver also.

32

Photograph 3. Rectangular Tray with Rounded Corners Decorated with Gold-Leaf Sprays

Place stencil No. F at the end center of the floor of the tray. Refer to Photograph 2. Stencil with silver powder on the tips of the flower petals, leaving the center dark and shadowy. Place the same stencil in two places along the long sides of the tray. Judge the placing by referring to the photograph on page 28 as to the proper position. Stencil in the same manner with silver, leaving a dark center.

Place stencil No. E to the left of flower No. F and stencil with light gold powder on the tips of the petals and red bronze powder in the center. Repeat this unit to the right of No. F.

Repeat this stenciling of two flowers around every flower No. F, making six groups on the floor of the tray. Add the stenciled center No. G to flower No. F with red bronze powder.

The leaf unit No. D is placed once at each end of each flower group and stenciled in deep gold powder. Stencil unit No. H is scattered among the flower groupings to fill in spaces, forming a continuous border. This also is done with deep gold powder. Set the tray aside to dry for at least forty-eight hours. When the tray is thoroughly dry, wash it well with water to remove all excess gold powder. Dry with a soft clean cloth.

Use black varnish medium to paint over all silver flowers No. A on the gold band. Paint these in smoothly and carefully for no erasures can be made. While you are waiting for these to dry to the tacky stage, use black varnish medium to paint the veins in the large silver leaves No. B, and to touch up, with small lines, the tips of these leaves on the shadow sides. Test black flowers occasionally to see whether they have reached the tacky stage. When they are tacky, stencil the centers with No. C stencil and light gold powder. After all centers are finished pick up with velvet finger red bronze powder and rub a red smudge over these centers.

Using a small quill brush, draw the fine stems of the small sprays of leaves interspersed among the flowers and large leaves with black paint. The small leaves are painted with one stroke of a medium size quill brush and green paint (Prussian blue, chrome yellow medium, raw umber and white). Make this paint fairly dark so that it will show against the gold-leaf background. If there is a chance of smudging the wet paint while working, we suggest that this final painting be done in stages so as to permit the drying of some parts before proceeding with others.

Place a small gold stripe between the edge of the gold band and the edge of the rim of the tray. Another small gold stripe should be placed on the floor of the tray one-quarter inch from the edge of the floor. Finish the tray with at least six coats of varnish. Refer to Chapter XI for directions. The various units of this pattern may also be used to decorate boxes, smaller trays and panels on simple chairs.

Photograph 4. Octagonal or Coffin Lid Tray

Octagonal Tray or Coffin Lid Tray

Octagonal trays were decorated in both primitive and classic designs, depending upon the period and style of tray. Early trays of the better type were decorated with beautiful gold-leaf borders, both on the rim and floor. Some were painted with center panels of landscapes. Later trays were done in a more simple manner with borders that were a combination of stenciling and free-hand painting. The country tinsmiths made a simple tray, often with a seam in the middle, in order to use small pieces of tin. These were quite simply painted with brush stroke patterns in a primitive style.

The octagonal tray shown on page 35 combines the gold-leaf technique of decoration and free-hand bronze painting. This tray measures fourteen by twenty inches with a rim two inches wide. Have your tray blackened, and protected by a coat of varnish. When this is thoroughly dry, rub the surface lightly with waterproof sandpaper No. 600 and water until perfectly smooth. Wash off and dry thoroughly. Buff the entire tray lightly with 4/0 steel wool. Sprinkle with talcum powder and wipe off with a dry cloth. Make sure that all steel wool particles are removed. Gold leaf must be laid on a very smooth, clean surface.

With a ruler and white chalk conté pencil measure and draw lines to define the sections for the patterns and the gold bands. Refer to the photograph on page 35. The band on the rim is one and a half inches wide, equally spaced from the outer edge and the floor edge of the tray. This leaves a quarter-inch margin on both sides of the band. Measure in from the edge of the floor one-quarter inch and draw a line around the floor of the tray. Measure in one and a half inches and draw another line. This defines the width of the band on the floor. Mark the diagonal lines at the corners which separate the areas to be covered with the different patterns.

Trace (using lithopone paper) the parts that are to be covered with gold leaf, the long sides of the rim and also the detail around the handle holes. On the tray floor, trace only the corners.

With varnish medium or gold size, paint in the corner bands on the rim, the long side bands and ends on the floor, smoothly and evenly. Refer to Chapter III for complete instructions. Large areas should be covered with gold size first as they require more time to reach the tacky stage. Paint in the smaller areas, such as the detail design on the long side of the rim, and diagonal corners of the floor last. Allow the size to dry to the tacky stage and then cover with gold leaf. This work may be done in sections at different times so as to enable you to handle your tray without marring previous work.

36

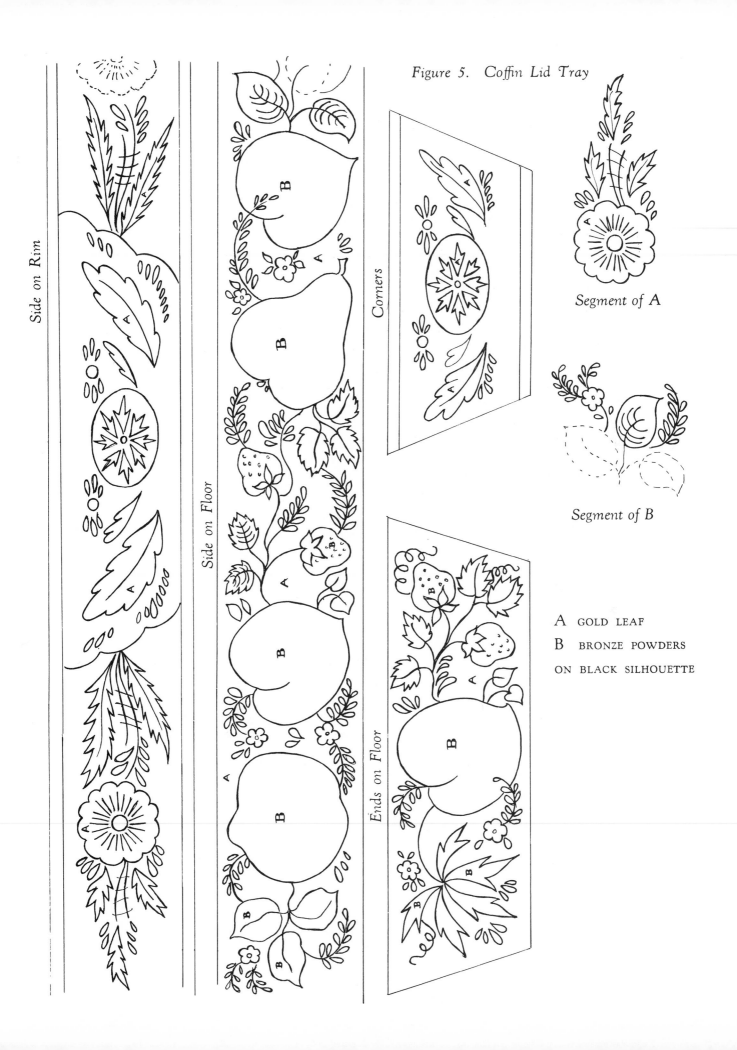

Figure 5. Coffin Lid Tray

Side on Rim

Side on Floor

Corners

Ends on Floor

Segment of A

Segment of B

A GOLD LEAF
B BRONZE POWDERS
ON BLACK SILHOUETTE

After the gold leaf is applied, wait for several hours, then remove the excess gold with a soft wad of cotton. Use a single etcher (an 8H pencil sharpened to a fine point) to mark the main lines as designated on the pattern. With a two- or three-point etcher, etch the shaded areas. All etching should be done on the same day the gold is applied. Then allow tray to dry for a week or more.

Cover the gold parts with varnish to protect them and allow to dry twenty-four hours or more. After this is dry trace your pattern on the gold bands with lithopone prepared transfer paper. It will be a little difficult to see your pattern, but we have found the lithopone to be better than graphite paper. Always trace patterns neatly, making sure that they are well drawn and that no extra meaningless lines are present to be eradicated later. A patched job is not always successful and it is better to work in a neat, clean fashion. This means keeping your work as free from dust particles as possible, for every little particle will mar the surface of gold leaf.

The fruits and large leaves are painted in with black varnish medium and a medium size quill brush. This is set aside to reach the tacky stage. Have your palette of gold and colored bronzes ready. Use either a velvet-wrapped finger or a dry quill brush to apply the dry bronze powders on the light areas of the fruit. A bit of red bronze powder is used for the blush on the fruit and for the strawberries. Leave the edges of the fruit and berries dark by using the bronze powder sparingly. Use matt green bronze powder on the leaves.

India ink is used to draw in the stems and the veins of the leaves, and also the tiny curlicues.

Mix a dark green of Prussian blue, raw umber, chrome yellow medium and white to paint the tiny leaves with one brush stroke each. Use white for the tiny flowers with a dot of vermilion for the centers.

Gold-leaf work may be corrected around the fuzzy edges by using a crow quill pen and India ink to draw around the edges and to sharpen and straighten them.

Apply gold stripes as shown in the photograph on page 35 made of varnish medium and gold-bronze powder. The corner bands of gold are striped with black paint one-fourth inch from the edges. A chain is made of black lines through the center of the band, and a larger chain is made of vermilion, overlapping the small black chain.

After your tray is completely dry give it at least six coats of good spar varnish. Refer to Chapter XI for directions on finishing trays. This design may be used on a tray slightly larger or smaller than the size given on page 37. Parts of this pattern may be used on rectangular trays with rounded corners. The bands may be placed on the long sides of the rim and the end sections of the rim, leaving the rounded corners for lattice work in old white. The striping should be done in old white. No design is used on the floor. This is decorated with a quarter-inch gold stripe placed about three-eighths to one-half inch in from the bend of the tray. An eighth inch from this wide stripe, place a very small gold stripe. Finish the tray by placing a gold stripe (small) one-eighth inch from the outer edge of the tray.

The various parts of this pattern may be used on perpendicular sides of boxes. A cluster of fruit and flowers may decorate the top, leaving the conventional parts for the sides of the boxes. Always use striping to complete the decoration. An occasional vermilion stripe, or soft green, old blue or yellow gives added interest.

Oblong Lace-Edge Tray, Tortoise-Shell Background

Photograph 5

Queen Anne Tray

CHAPTER VI

Queen Anne Tray

The tray on page 40 with the curved edge, designated as Queen Anne, is restored with an authentic pattern which came from an old tray in the author's possession. The original tray measures twelve by fourteen inches. The background is black and the large center rose is a delicate pink while the smaller flowers which encircle it are of a deeper pink.

Transfer the pattern to the tray with lithopone paper. Paint all green leaves with a medium gray-green (Prussian blue, raw umber, chrome yellow medium and white). Dark blue-greens may be added in the shadows and yellow-greens may be added near the tips for lights.

Mix alizarin crimson, burnt umber and varnish medium. Put a generous smudge of this in the center of one of the small flowers. With a square-tipped quill brush pick up some thin white (white, raw umber and varnish medium), and begin at the outer edge of the petal, drawing the brush from the tip of the petal to the center of the flower and back to the outer edge for another stroke to complete the petal. Each time your brush will pick up some of the red center which mixes with the white and is carried to the tip of the petal. You will be surprised and delighted with the way this technique produces variation in the colors. If it mixes too much, clean your brush, dip into the white and start a new petal. After all petals are finished, renew the center by placing more red (alizarin and burnt umber) there and encircling it with yellow dots. Repeat this on all of the small flowers, adding more and more white, so that there is a gradation of color tone from dark to light, the last flowers on the left being the lightest.

For the buds, place a smudge of dark color at the base, and white at the tip. Blend with a dry brush.

For the rose in the center, place a dark spot of color in the deep center of the cup and more dark color around the underside of the cup. Place bits of white near the edges of the unfolding petals at the bottom. Blend the dark with the light, patting it with the side of a dry brush or with the ball of your finger, leaving darks in the shadows and lights on the edges. The blending will make a middle tone where these two colors meet. Place a blob of white on the upper edge near the top of the cup and blend with the dark color under the cup. Refer to the diagram for placing of lights

41

Figure 6.

Border

Queen Anne Tray

A   GOLD
B   PINK
C   GREEN

and darks. Allow this basic painting to dry. There should be no sharp edges — they should be feathery and transparent. Refer to diagram on page 16 for the shading of a rose.

Twenty-four hours later, repeat this basic painting with the same light colors and dark colors. While the paint is wet, draw in the white lines to outline the petals. With a dry brush, blend into the background paint, especially in the shadows, leaving a bit here and there of the white line, to accent the edges of the petals.

White accents may now be added to the small flowers. Mix a bit of raw umber with the white to draw the veins in the leaves and to accent the stems. Paint the scroll border with gold-bronze powder and varnish medium. Stripe around the edge of the tray with gold. Finishing instructions are to be found in Chapter XI.

Round Lace-Edge Tray

Lace-edge trays, sometimes called trays with perforated borders, were among the earliest made in Pontypool. They were usually prepared with tortoise-shell background and were further decorated with bouquets of flowers, garlands of ribbon, butterflies, birds and fruit. These trays belong to the eighteenth century.

The design given on page 46 is suitable for a tray from ten to twelve inches in diameter. It is similar but not identical to the photograph on page 44. To prepare a tortoise-shell ground, start with a clean unpainted tray. Give it a coat of metal primer, and twenty-four hours later rub with waterproof sandpaper No. 600 until perfectly smooth. Rinse off and dry carefully. Paint with one coat of japan black (japan black mixed with turpentine to the consistency of thin coffee cream). Add one teaspoon varnish to one-fourth cup of paint. This will be sufficient for one coat. Twenty-four hours later cover with a coat of quick-drying varnish. When this is tacky, lay several pieces of palladium leaf at intervals on the floor of the tray. Palladium is to be preferred to silver as it will not tarnish. Let dry for several days.

Cover the tray with a coat of varnish that has been strongly colored with alizarin crimson from your artist's colors in tubes. The alizarin crimson will retard the drying, so again wait longer than the usual twenty-four hours for this to dry.

Several days later, cover the tray with a coat of black japan mixed the same as the first coat of black. While the paint is wet, take a crumpled stiff cloth (a piece of an old sheet), and with a twisting motion lift out the

Photograph 6. Round Lace-Edge Trays

black paint over the red tinted palladium. The red will show through, giving the effect suggested. It is described in old pamphlets as "tortoise-shell." It would be well to protect this background with a coat of varnish after twenty-four hours. When dry, buff lightly with 4/0 steel wool to dull the surface before beginning the painting of the pattern.

To paint the pattern, begin with the leaves, stems and tendrils, in soft gray-green (blue, raw umber, yellow and white). Blend darker green into the shadows. A creamy white is used to accent the edges of the leaves and to mark the veins. Use old white (white and umber) as an underpainting for all small flowers and buds.

Paint in the large zinnia flower with old white (white with more umber than usual) in a deep tone, leaving the edges quite thin. Paint morning glories in old white, blending Prussian blue into the edges of the flower. Refer to the diagram of lights and shadows on flowers, page 18. Paint the rose in Venetian red in the dark parts, adding white to the light parts. Refer also to the diagram of flowers on page 16. Set the tray aside to dry for twenty-four hours.

On the next painting, go over the greens where they may seem too thin. Touch up the shadows and make corrections where necessary. Glaze the large stems with a tiny bit of burnt umber and alizarin crimson. Float Prussian blue and varnish medium on the shadow sides of the forget-me-nots. Put a touch of raw umber with varnish medium and a bit of terre verte on the bell-shaped flowers for shadows.

Go over the blue parts of the morning-glory, accenting the dark parts. The purpose of this second coat is to enable you to do more subtle blending than can be accomplished on the first coat.

Accent a few light places on the edge of the flower by using a thin hairline of white. Float a bit of soft yellow (yellow, raw umber, white and varnish medium) in the throat of the flower. Make three brush strokes of alizarin crimson for the stamens.

For the large white flower, paint the entire surface with *old white* in a very deep tone to which some terre verte has been added. The center, the edges, and back part should have the most shadow. Paint the shadow parts darker. Be sure that the edges of the flower have not become loaded with paint.

With a large quill brush and old white, paint in the petals, beginning on the back of the flower where it is darkest. As you proceed around the edge, begin to lighten the petals (by adding clean white) so that they will be their lightest in the middle front, but not a pure white. Pure white must be reserved for the highest light which will be near the center of the flower. Start the second row of petals at the back, letting them overlap

45

A WHITE — ZINNIA
B BLUE — MORNING-GLORY
C CRIMSON — ROSE
D GREEN — LEAVES

Figure 7. Round Lace-Edge Tray. (Not identical to Photograph 6.)

the lower row, and proceed to paint around the flower as in the first row. Continue painting each row until you reach the center of the flower. Paint the center yellow, mellowed with burnt umber and a bit of alizarin, giving it an orange tinge. Use chrome yellow light to make the little brush strokes which surround the center.

Paint the rose again the same as the first coat. Mark the petals with thin white and blend with the wet paint in the dark areas, leaving a few lines to accent the light edges of the petals. Accent the center with a few dark brush strokes and paint a few deep yellow dots for stamens. The rose may be made lighter by adding more white to your design, using the Venetian only for a suggestion of depth and shadow.

In order to explain the painting of a rose more clearly, think of it as shaped like a bird's nest. Experiment on a piece of black cardboard. (Be sure the cardboard is not absorbent — shellac it before trying to paint on it.) The rose is almost oval in shape and should be shadowed around all edges but kept darker at the top since that part is farthest away. As objects recede, they become more shadowy. Near the top, paint a large oval shape in dark red to represent the scooped-out center of the nest. Now add a few unfolding petals around the bottom of this bird-nest shape. This under-painting serves two purposes. It covers the black background and gives us a surface upon which to work; also, it blocks in a pattern of lights and shadows for our future flower. Avoid ridges of paint by patting this underpainting with a dry brush or with the ball of the little finger. *Be careful* that you do not blend the colors into one monotonous tone. Pat the darks, then wipe your brush or finger, and then pat the lights.

Twenty-four hours later, repaint the rose in the exact, same colors. This will give us material to use in blending and when drawing the details. The white lines must be a part of the flower by being blended with the paint, leaving a line so thin that we do not see it as a line but as a fine edge.

Place the border around the edge of the floor of the tray. Paint this with varnish medium and a bit of gold-bronze powder. When tacky apply gold leaf. Some lace-edge trays had the lace painted gold but others were left black. It is a matter of your own choice. Finish with six coats of varnish as directed in Chapter XI.

Oblong Lace-Edge Tray

Prepare your tray with the tortoise-shell background described in the section on "Round Lace-Edge Tray," Chapter VI. Paint all stems and leaves in a medium blue-green (Prussian blue, chrome yellow medium, white and raw umber). Accent the stems with a bit of lighter green.

Figure 8.   Oblong Lace-Edge Tray

Paint all tiny flowers and buds in old white, including the daisy type flowers in the corners of the tray. The three large petals of the large flower are also old white and the three small petals are soft old yellow (yellow, burnt umber and white). Make an underpainting of vermilion on the rosebud.

Twenty-four hours later go over the greens to make sure that the black background does not show through. With old white draw in the veins and the large brush stroke which accents one side of the leaf. An accent line of this color is placed on the upper side of all green brush-stroke leaves of this pattern.

With burnt umber and varnish medium float some shadows on the white petals of the white flower and make shadow brush strokes radiating from the center of the flower. Use the same burnt umber to make large shadow strokes on the leaves; stamens are deep yellow.

Glaze one side of the daisies and all buds with a floating color of blue (Prussian blue and varnish medium). This blue should be on the tips of the buds only. Mix alizarin crimson, burnt umber and varnish medium to use as a glaze (or floating color) over the rosebud, fading out to clear varnish in the highlights and intensifying the color in the shadow. Float thin white over the highlight of the rosebud.

After this is dry, paint the green calyx of the rosebud and accent in the same manner as the other green leaves and stems. The fine gold line border should be placed near the edge of the floor of the tray, and should be made of gold leaf. Finish with six coats of varnish and rub down with pumice and oil. Refer to Chapter XI for directions.

Photograph 7. Chippendale Tray with Mother-of-Pearl

CHAPTER VII

Chippendale Tray Decorated in Gold Leaf and Mother-of-Pearl

Early Chippendale or Gothic trays were decorated with elaborate designs, floral centers, fountains, exotic birds. They often had dusted gold backgrounds varying from the dark golds in the shadows to the lighter golds in the important highlights, focusing the attention and interest on an exotic bird or fountain. Pale gold cloud formations lent depth to the design. An occasional butterfly or small insect was added for a bit of whimsey.

We have selected a design for a tray fifteen inches by eighteen inches, which includes gold leaf, mother-of-pearl and some hand-painting. Genuine mother-of-pearl is hard to find but can be imitated readily. See directions in Chapter III. Before beginning on your design, make sure that your tray is dry. The protecting coat of varnish that you put over the last coat of black should have had at least two weeks to dry. When you are ready to decorate your tray, rub off all specks of dust with black waterproof sandpaper No. 600 and water. Wash and dry the tray thoroughly. Use 4/0 steel wool to buff the tray lightly and thoroughly.

Do not use tack cloth but dust the tray with talcum powder and then wipe off the talcum with a dry soft cloth. Talcum will help to prevent the gold leaf from sticking to the background where it is not wanted.

From this point on, be careful not to touch the surface of your tray with sticky fingers. It is better to handle your tray by placing your fingers under the edge when lifting it.

Trace your pattern on your tray with lithopone powdered paper. Use white shellac to paint in all areas where you wish to place the pearl. Also, paint the underside of the pearl with white shellac and set it aside to dry for at least thirty minutes.

Repeat the shellac on the pattern and on the pearl and immediately place the pearl on the tray in the designated places. Press down firmly with your finger. Set aside to dry. If your shellac was used too sparingly, there may be air pockets under the pearl which will cause it to look spotty. However, too much shellac will be equally bad as it takes a long time to

Figure 9. Center of Chippendale Tray with Mother-of-Pearl
X. Pearl Leaves and Pearl Centers. Remainder Done in Gold Leaf

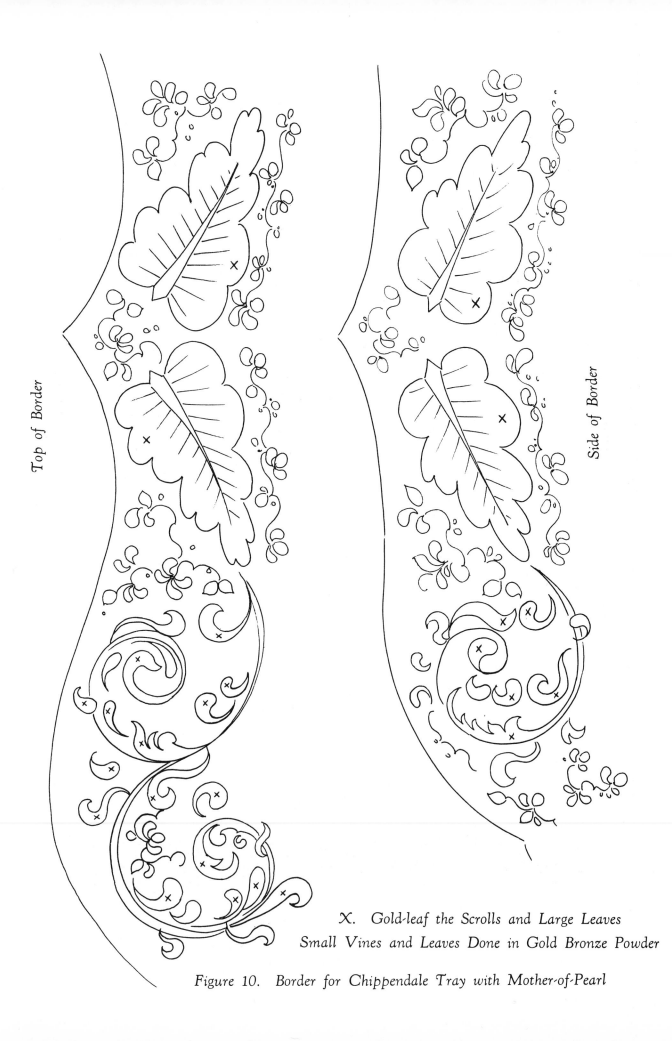

Top of Border

Side of Border

X. Gold-leaf the Scrolls and Large Leaves
Small Vines and Leaves Done in Gold Bronze Powder

Figure 10. Border for Chippendale Tray with Mother-of-Pearl

dry. So press the pearl down firmly and wipe away any excess shellac. This has to be done quickly as shellac dries at once when exposed to the air.

A piece of tissue paper may be placed over the mother-of-pearl area and stuck down with masking tape while you work on your border. Start at one point on the border, and continue around the tray (see page 53), painting all sections and parts of the scrolls as you go along, using a medium quill brush, service seal or gold size and a very small amount of gold powder. The gold powder is used only to make the brush strokes more visible. Keep the scrolls round and graceful, remembering that all scroll borders are based on a design pattern, combining the letters S and C. Sometimes these letters are inverted and again they are placed back to back. However, if you keep these two letters in mind when painting, it will help you to follow through on some of the longer strokes with a more graceful form to the design.

When you have painted one-fourth of the border, test the first part with your finger to see if it is tacky. If the gold size is still too wet, paint more of the border, stopping frequently to test the first part for the application of gold leaf. Lay the gold leaf only as far as the proper stage of tackiness exists. Stop and wait for the next section to dry. You may continue to paint with gold size, but do not forget to stop and test the size where you left off the laying of the gold. When the border scrolls are finished wipe off the excess gold leaf with a soft wad of cotton. The small leaves and vines, interspersed among the scrolls, should be painted later with deep gold-bronze powder.

Uncover the center design on the tray and apply gold leaf to the areas designated, the curlicues and the few leaves and flower spots among the curlicues. Outline the large leaves in gold. Should any gold adhere to the background, remove it with a cotton-wrapped toothpick dipped in varnish medium.

Allow the tray to dry a week or more. Dust well. Remove any specks of gold and wipe off the tray with a soft wet cloth. Dry well. Give the tray a protective coat of varnish. Allow to dry.

Paint the pearl leaves with a transparent green (viridian and burnt umber mixed with varnish medium). In the darker areas use more burnt umber and in the lighter areas make the green quite brilliant, leaving the lightest portion untinted.

Paint the rosebud with alizarin crimson and varnish medium. Paint the stems and the details around the bud with opaque green (Prussian blue, raw umber, chrome yellow medium and white). Use alizarin crimson, burnt umber and white to paint the flowers. Make the lower flower darker than the flower on the left. This flower should be a soft pale pink.

54

Draw in the details on the pearl leaves with India ink and pen. The details of the large leaves in the border are also drawn with pen and ink. Paint a burnt umber stroke down the center of these leaves. Now place a narrow gold bronze stripe around the tray one-eighth inch from the edge.

Build up the surface of the tray with eight to ten coats of varnish, allowing each coat to dry forty-eight hours or more. Lightly buff the tray with steel wool between varnish coats. After the fifth coat use waterproof black sandpaper No. 600 and water to rub the tray, removing all specks of dust. This may be done again after the seventh coat. Refer to Chapter XI for instructions on finishing.

Chippendale Tray with Blue Center

The Chippendale Tray with the blue center pictured on page 55 has not been restored. This is an authentic tray over one hundred years old. The center design is in fairly good condition, showing the bright clear colors which were used at that period. Time and rust have worn away most of the border. There is just enough border left to enable us to make a tracing for a record, so that we may restore it at some future time. This original old tray measures fourteen inches by seventeen inches.

Make an outline of the center section by tracing from your pattern. Paint this panel old blue, a color made by mixing bulletin blue japan paint with turpentine, one-half teaspoon of varnish and just enough raw umber to soften the blue. Paint in with a second coat twenty-four hours later. When this is dry, cover with a protective coat of varnish. Allow to dry thoroughly. Then buff the tray lightly with steel wool. Dust with talcum powder and wipe off with soft dry cloth. Trace the complete pattern on the tray, using lithopone powdered paper.

Start at one point of your tray and continue in one direction to paint in all scrolls with varnish medium or gold size mixed with a very small amount of gold-bronze powder. When you have painted one-fourth of the border, test the first part with your finger to determine whether it has reached the right tacky stage for applying the gold leaf. If it is too sticky, continue to paint your scroll border, stopping occasionally to test the first part for tackiness.

When your scrolls have reached the tacky stage, lay the gold leaf as described in Chapter III. Complete the scroll border around the center panel and on the urn also at this time. Set the tray aside for two or three weeks for the gold leaf to become dry. Excess gold may be wiped off with a very soft wad of cotton. Buff the gold lightly with cotton to give it added luster.

Figure 11. Chippendale Tray with Blue Center. Center Design

*Border of Chippendale Tray
with Blue Center
(upper right corner)*

*Border of Chippendale Tray
with Blue Center
(lower left corner)*

Figure 12

A few brush strokes of burnt umber should be applied to the urn for shadows. Paint all leaves and stems in light chrome green and medium chrome green mixed. Paint the tiny fuchsia flowers in cadmium red medium and the small five-petal flowers in old white (white with raw umber), with red centers. For the large white flower in the urn, paint in a large olive green center. With a large quill brush and old white, paint the petals, beginning at the outer edge and drawing the brush toward the center with one long brush stroke. Two brush strokes should be sufficient to paint each petal. Do not attempt to fill in an outline with numerous small strokes. Make your brush work for you. Do not blend the white with the green. Make the petals stop at the edge of the green center. Leave this flower until another time for the finishing touches.

For the rose, make an underpainting of thin white with the tiniest bit of raw umber to soften it. This must be very smooth painting, almost transparent and "filmy" with no thick paint on the edges.

Twenty-four hours later you may start again on your leaves. Mix a soft clear yellow of chrome yellow light, a touch of raw umber and varnish medium. Paint the centers of the leaves, beginning at the center vein and drawing your brush stroke outward to follow the line of smaller veins. Make complete brush strokes that feather out to points, making the zig-zag edge as shown on the pattern. The same yellow is used to accent the smaller leaves. When this has dried, one long brush stroke of burnt umber is drawn down the center of each leaf, and on top of this fine yellow lines mark the veins.

Cover the large white six-petal flower with varnish medium and work in a tiny bit of alizarin crimson on the lower edge of the petals. A small dash of alizarin crimson accents the center edge of each petal. Mix a bright yellow of chrome yellow medium and varnish medium and encircle the green center with a ring of yellow dots. Place one large dot in the center of the green. Accent the circle of yellow dots and the large center dot with red dots made of alizarin crimson and varnish medium.

Cover the rose with varnish medium and blend in alizarin crimson (which has been modified with burnt umber) on the top side of the rose. With a large quill brush, blend and work in the petals of the rose by adding white to varnish medium and placing each petal carefully. Remember to work in the back and center parts first, finishing with the large petals in the foreground. These last petals should be almost white, since they are painted over the lightest part of the underpainting. A few dashes of alizarin crimson to deepen the center should be applied last.

With a large square-tipped brush place a few large strokes of burnt umber and varnish medium at intervals on the scroll borders to soften the

Photograph 9
Chippendale Tray.   Circa 1800.   Brushed Gold Background

brilliance of the gold leaf. A few large, thin swishes of burnt umber should also be placed on the tips of the large green leaves.

Last, place tiny yellow dots of chrome yellow light in the center of the rose and all other flowers. Stripe the edge of the tray with gold-bronze powder and varnish medium.

Varnish with at least two coats before using steel wool. To antique the tray, add a tiny particle of burnt umber to the varnish used for the third coat. If this is not enough add a tiny bit of black (ivory black artist's oil color) to the fourth coat of varnish. If one or two applications of antiquing are not sufficient, still another may be added, but too much antiquing cannot be rectified — *so be careful!* The tray will look still softer in tone after the final rubdown with pumice and oil. See Chapter XI for finishing.

Chippendale Tray with Brushed Gold Background

For this small tray twelve inches by fifteen inches (see page 60), we have selected a design suitable in size, employing a technique not heretofore discussed, the brushed gold background.

First, the tray must be perfectly smooth, for every little blemish will show through the gold powder. Have the room where you are working as *dust free* as you can possibly make it. Varnish the tray and set it aside to become nearly dry. On a clean palette arrange at least three shades of gold-bronze powder, light, medium and dark (which may be statuary bronze). Make a pounce out of a large wad of cotton covered with velvet. With this pounce pick up from your palette some of the lightest gold and with a circular motion dust in the lightest area, which should be a little above the true center of the tray. Do not have very much powder on the pounce, for it must fade off before you have covered a third of the floor area. Then pick up the medium shade of gold and set the pounce down on the light area and gradually work out to the parts immediately surrounding the light gold center. Let this gold fade off into the black background. Last, pick up the dark bronze on the pounce and blend it from the medium area into the darks. Each shade of gold overlaps the preceding one and should make a satisfactory blending. Let the tray dry at least forty-eight hours. Wash off the excess gold powder with water. Give the entire tray a protective coat of varnish.

Twenty-four hours later, lightly buff the tray with steel wool. Transfer your pattern to the tray. Paint in all green leaves and stems with a medium green (Prussian blue, raw umber, chrome yellow medium and white). This will be your darkest tone which is used for the darkest part of the leaves

Match 2 and 3 in scroll border
to Figure 14 drawing

Figure 13. Center Design for Chippendale Tray. Brushed Gold Background

A GOLD   D GREEN
B PINK   E YELLOW
C WHITE

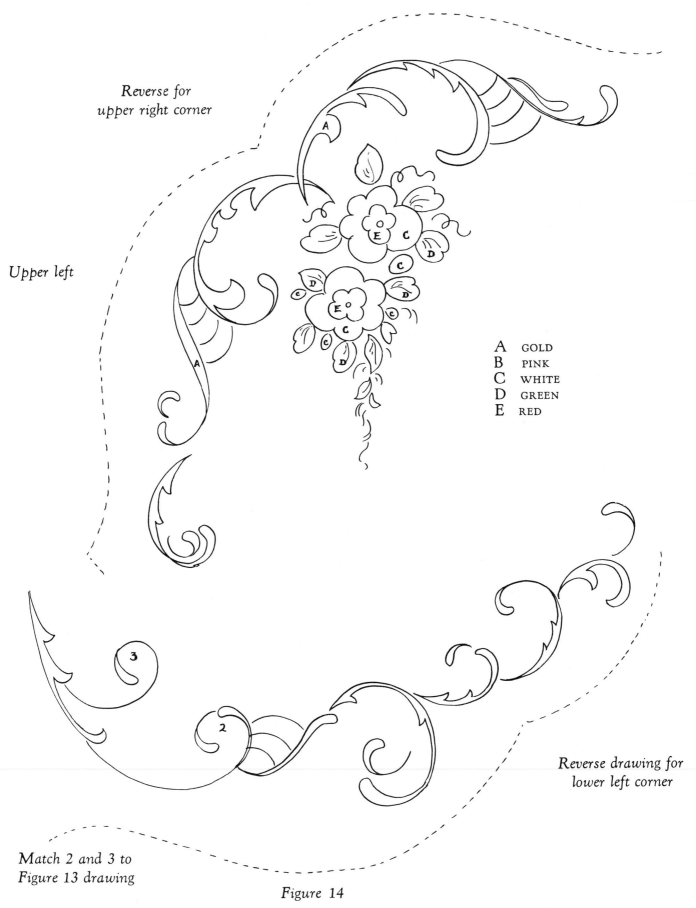

Reverse for
upper right corner

Upper left

A GOLD
B PINK
C WHITE
D GREEN
E RED

Reverse drawing for
lower left corner

Match 2 and 3 to
Figure 13 drawing

Figure 14
Border Design for Chippendale Tray.   Brushed Gold Background

near the flowers. Gradually lighten the green toward the tips by adding white and a small amount of yellow. Blend the colors until the leaves are smooth.

Paint in the large eight-petal flower in old white (white with raw umber), shading the flower darker in the center. The small flowers on the upper right and left near the border are also painted in old white. Paint in the remainder of the small flowers with alizarin crimson which has been modified with vermilion and burnt umber. Blend in white for highlights.

Note: Paint in the rose with old white and alizarin crimson. Add burnt umber to the alizarin for the deepest color, which will be in the cup of the rose and along the lower edges. Blend to a smooth soft tone, leaving the edges of the flower very thin.

Let this first painting become thoroughly dry before painting the final details. Paint in the border scrolls with gold-bronze powder and varnish medium. When it reaches the tacky stage, dust with dry gold-bronze powder, using a velvet-wrapped finger to pick up the powder and to apply it. Stripe the edge with gold-bronze powder mixed with varnish medium.

Twenty-four hours later the finishing touches may be added to the flowers. Touch up the green leaves, making certain that the green paint has covered the area of the leaves. Mix a dark green and apply brush strokes in the shadows. Paint in the veins with soft pale green that is almost white. Accent a few edges and points of the leaves.

Accent the eight petals of the large white flower with white. For the center tiny yellow dots are placed over the entire center, densely on the upper side and more sparsely on the lower side. Burnt sienna and burnt umber are mixed to make the dark dots, which are thickly painted on the lower side and scattered thinly on the upper side. One large area of dark dots in the center gives it accent.

The white flowers in the border have a dark red center (alizarin crimson and burnt umber), over which is painted a large yellow dot. The small red flowers in the center design should be covered with varnish, and into this blend a bit of alizarin crimson. Touch the upper edges of the flowers and buds with a thin line of white for accent.

Cover the rose with another coat of paint exactly as the first tints and shadows were done. With a fine quill brush and white paint that has been thinned with varnish, draw the petals, beginning with the ones on the back side of the flower. With a dry brush blend the colors to the shape of the petal. Continue to draw in the petals and blend until the entire flower has been shaped. It takes much practice to make a rose that pleases us. If your first attempt does not satisfy you, wipe it off with a dry cloth. Wipe toward the center of the flower so as to prevent the paint from being smudged on the background.

64

Try painting the rose again, putting the dark paint deep in the cup of the rose, and the light on the near side of the cup near the top. Study the diagram as to the placing of lights and shadows. A few yellow dots in the center finish the rose.

For other roses we suggest light red, or Venetian red instead of alizarin crimson. For a yellow rose, use yellow ochre and white with burnt umber and a touch of burnt sienna in the shadows.

Vermilion and white can be used to make a very pale pink rose. Leave the stems dark where they are placed behind flowers, leaves and other stems. Accent with white at other places where the light strikes them. Finish the tray with at least six coats of varnish and rub down as described in Chapter XI in the section on finishing trays.

Photograph 10

An Authentic Old Tray with Mother-of-Pearl. Restored by Author

CHAPTER VIII

Glass Painting: Clock Glass

Glass paintings were used to decorate clock doors and mirrors, and sometimes the lids of boxes and lap desks. Some elaborate pictures used on papier-mâché boxes had parts of the design backed with mother-of-pearl to give added luminosity.

Use only the thinnest glass for your glass painting. Varnish one side of the glass and set it aside to dry. Be sure your glass is the *correct size* for your clock, as you will be taking a great risk cutting it after it is painted.

Copy the design (see page 69) on frosted acetate with pen and drawing ink. Place this tracing face down on a white cardboard and on top of the tracing place the glass with the varnished side on top. Remember, you paint on the reverse side of the glass!

In the clock glass the lines are all drawn on the varnished glass with pen and India ink. If necessary, use a ruler for the straight lines of the building. Work for perfection, since every careless line is there to stay. Draw all the details of the border at this time also. After the ink is dry, an hour or so, varnish the small part of the border and the small oval open-ing in the center of the glass. When this reaches the tacky stage, dust with gold powder, applied with a velvet-covered finger. Wipe off the excess gold powder with a damp cloth (being careful not to touch any inked lines on the picture). Cover the outer portion of the border with black varnish medium.

For the landscape, paint the areas in the foreground first — the foliage of the foreground and the grass areas, then the trees, being careful that each color stays within its boundaries.

Paint the shadows on the building. Use light gray for the roof, a little deeper gray on the area behind the columns. White is used for the columns. Dark red goes on the chimney. All of this painting is done on the varnished side of the glass but the other side is the one which will show the finished picture. So lift the glass occasionally and examine it to make sure that your colors are being placed correctly. Paint in all details except the sky and water which will be last. The hill on the horizon should be a hazy gray blue. The windows in the building will be the darkest area. The house, itself, is pale gray.

Photograph 11. Terry Clock. Owned by Mrs. Howard Amidon

Figure 15. *Clock Glass: Terry Clock*

Figure 16. Mirror Glass

The grass should be yellow-green. The foliage will be a variation of green tones with some burnt umber shadings in the darker areas, including the shadow areas on the trees. After this part has dried, mix a soft old blue (blue, raw umber, white) for the sky, starting with the darkest at the very top of the glass — making it lighter at the horizon by adding more white. Medium blue is used in the shadow parts of the water, varying to white where it reflects the sky.

All the paints used for the colors in this picture are your oil colors in tubes mixed with varnish medium. This will tend to make it semi-transparent in some places. A second coat of the same color may be applied after the first one is thoroughly dry.

Glass Painting: Mirror Glass

The picture for a mirror is painted in the same manner as the clock glass, with one exception. Instead of using India ink to draw the lines, use burnt umber and Van Dyke brown with varnish medium and apply it with a very small brush. The shadows should be painted in burnt umber and varnish medium at this time. (See page 70.) Allow the lines time to dry thoroughly.

In this picture paint the figures in the foreground and the geese first. The boat, the houses and trees may be painted also where they do not touch any of the figures. The roofs of the houses are red in the sun (Venetian red); use some burnt umber with the red in the shadow areas. The houses are old white on the front, and have burnt umber added to the white for the shadow sides. After these parts are dry, paint the green trees back of the houses, the green hills light in the foreground (light green with yellow added), and more shadowy as they recede to the horizon. After twenty-four hours paint dark blue shadows on the water near the shore. The water should be softened blue (add raw umber and white) in the foreground, fading to a grayish light blue at the horizon. The deepest blue of the sky is at the top of the picture, fading out to a pale grayish blue near the water.

Photograph 12. Hitchcock Chair

CHAPTER IX

Hitchcock Chair

Hitchcock chairs were manufactured in Connecticut around 1820. There were many different styles of backs: plain panel, cornucopia, eagle, turtle back, crown back and others. Some had wooden seats (for kitchen use) and others had cane and rush seats. A number have been well preserved over the years and from them we have been able to trace the beautiful old designs. Today, reproductions of these chairs are being made on the same location in Riverton, Connecticut, where the early chairs were made, so it is now possible for you to have one or even a set to grace your home.

The design we have chosen (see page 74) came from an early chair. The panel to be decorated measures five and one-fourth inches wide by thirteen inches long.

Choose a bright clear day to do your stenciling. Have your chair prepared as directed in Chapter II. Cut your stencils very carefully, making sure that you have left enough margin around the edge of each unit. Mark them with numbers corresponding to the diagram. Arrange your palette of colored bronzes on a piece of velvet or velour, and have two or three squares of velvet (four inches by four inches) to use for applying the bronze powder. Make a pattern, of tracing paper, the exact size and shape of the panel of the chair. Locate the center by folding the paper in half. Mark the center (using paper pattern as a guide) of the panel on the chair with a dot of chalk, where it will not interfere with the stenciling.

Varnish this panel with slow-drying varnish. When it reaches the tacky stage place stencil No. A in the center of the panel. Wrap your index finger with a square of velvet, making sure it has no wrinkles on the ball of the finger. Secure it with a rubber band just tight enough to keep it from falling off your finger. Do not make it too tight. Dip into the palest gold powder mixed with a bit of silver, rub out the excess on a cloth pad, and apply the gold powder over the stencil covering all perforations solidly except the base. Stencil the base heavily in the center, fading out toward the ends. Then lift the stencil carefully and set it aside.

Place stencil No. B and rub deep gold very thinly over the entire silhouette pattern. Add a little extra gold in the center of the bowl. Stencil the fruits No. C and No. D in pale gold with silver highlights. Use a

73

Figure 17. Hitchcock Chair Design

A BOWL DETAIL   F GRAPE
B BOWL SILHOUETTE   G STEM
C PEACH   H SEAT
D MELON
E FLOWER

On Pillow

On Back Panel

different piece of velvet for the silver powder. Stencil the flowers No. E in deep gold. The highlights on the flowers are made with a tiny dry brush dipped into pale gold powder. They may also be made with a stump, such as is used in charcoal drawing. These may be bought at your art supply store. Place the stems No. G for the grapes next, and stencil in deep gold. The grapes are done, one at a time, placing the largest complete ones first, and filling in and around the first grapes to make a nicely shaped bunch. The lightest grapes should be done in pale gold gradually shading to deep gold in the background.

The leaves should be stenciled in deep gold mixed with a bit of dark copper. The shaded veins are stenciled with deep gold mixed with pale gold. Shaded veins are made by stenciling along the edge of a curved piece of architect's linen, permitting the gold powder to fade into shadow. Move the linen to a new location and repeat the shaded line. (The earliest and best chairs were stenciled in various shades of gold and silver. Later chairs had bits of color and colored bronzes added.)

For the stiles, the seat front, and the bolster top, the design is painted with a brush, and bronze powder mixed with varnish medium. Stripe the chair as indicated in the picture with yellow (chrome yellow medium, yellow ochre and raw umber and white). Thin with varnish medium and use a quill striper with hairs an inch and a half long. A wide stripe in gold should be painted around the decorated panel. Striping on the legs does not go entirely around the leg. About one-fourth of the leg is left bare as it does not show.

Hitchcock Chair Design (Reduced)

Before varnishing, wipe off the loose gold powder with a wet cloth. Dust the chair thoroughly and apply two or more coats of spar or floor varnish. When this is dry, rub well with steel wool to remove little rough specks. Wipe off chair, making sure to remove all bits of steel wool. Dust with tack cloth before applying a coat of rubbed effect varnish.

75

CHAPTER X

Four-Drawer Chest

Old pieces of furniture, which have no real antique value but have good lines and proportions, offer us an opportunity to exercise our originality in decoration, adding to their attractiveness and usefulness. Three- or four-drawer chests, such as pictured below, may be used in any room of the home. Choose the decorations to harmonize with the room in which it is to be used.

We suggest as basic ground colors: vermilion, soft dark green, dark brown, old yellow, maroon and any of the pastel tints. The design pictured may be used on any background with a slight change in value of the colors of the design.

Pine Four-Drawer Chest

Figure 18. Design for Four-Drawer Chest

A PINK
B YELLOW
C GREEN

Photograph 13.

Old Pennsylvania German Dower Chest. Painted by Raymond E. Krape

Paint the chest a soft gray-green. Use japan paint in medium green, add raw umber and white until you have the shade you desire. A very small amount of red will gray the paint, but add this color with caution. Two thin coats, spaced twenty-four hours apart, are better than one. After this has dried, give the chest a protective coat of varnish. Let dry thoroughly and buff lightly with steel wool 4/0.

Mark the stripes on the chest with a white conté chalk pencil. Stripe the drawers and ends with soft creamy yellow, made by adding white to yellow ochre. Stripe around the top, one inch from the edge.

Transfer the designs to the chest with lithopone prepared paper. Paint in all the leaves with green, a little darker than the background color (Prussian blue, raw umber, chrome yellow medium and white), using more varnish medium than usual to thin the paint. When it is tacky, use your velvet-wrapped finger to apply gold bronze powder to the larger leaves on the tips. Use varnish medium and gold bronze powder to paint in the curlicues. Draw veins in the leaves with black paint.

Use yellow ochre to paint the silhouette of one of the roses. While this is wet, use a large quill brush with white paint to brush in the petals with large strokes. These strokes should follow the contour of the rose. They will mix with the ochre paint as you work, giving a variation in tone from yellow ochre to light cream. Add more white for the final light strokes on the lightest part of the rose. Accent the center with a few strokes of yellow ochre and burnt umber. Add some yellow dots for stamens.

The other rose is painted in the same manner with the exception that we use Venetian red instead of yellow ochre. If this first painting has not covered the background color, touch up the flowers (twenty-four hours later) with the same flower colors. Paint the ends of the chest in the same manner.

When the flowers and leaves are dry cover the chest with two coats of good spar varnish. Rub lightly with fine sandpaper to remove any rough specks. Dust well. Wipe with a tack cloth before applying a coat of dull or rubbed effect varnish.

Pennsylvania German Dower Chest

The decorated dower chests and bride-boxes of the Pennsylvania Germans* remind us of the peasant furniture of central Europe. The colors were gay and fresh and the designs were simple. There was very little

---
* Popularly known as "Pennsylvania Dutch."

attempt made at modeling or shading. Age has made the colors more soft and mellow.

The motifs most used were flowers and birds. However, animals and figures were occasionally found. Birds, doves, parrots, eagles, horses, unicorns and other symbols were used along with inscriptions, initials and dates. Chests of this kind harmonize with simple furnishings and are useful for storage as well as being an ornamental addition to a room.

The chest pictured on page 78 is a restored one with a design in panels on the front and ends as well as the top. The ground color of the body of the chest is brown, a favorite color of the early chest decorators. The panels are old white and the designs are executed in green, red, yellow, brown and black. Small replicas of these dower chests would make nice trinket boxes. Choose various colors for backgrounds such as vermilion, blue, green or mottled backgrounds using two colors.

It is not possible to reproduce the pattern for this chest in our book as it is much too large. Try to sketch it free-hand. Do not worry if it seems crude, for that will add to its charm. The old chests were crude and no attempt was made to blend and shade the parts of the pattern.

When you have finished your design, give the chest a coat of varnish. When thoroughly dry, antique the chest with a mixture of raw and burnt umber (or Van Dyke brown) and turpentine. Mix a cupful of this, making it very thin. Add about three tablespoons of varnish. Paint this over the entire chest. Wipe it off with old cloths, leaving just enough on the chest to soften all the colors. Try it first on a scrap of painted wood to determine how fast it dries and the speed you will have to use when working on the chest.

After this is thoroughly dry you may varnish the chest as it will help to preserve your decoration. This coat of varnish should be followed by a coat of "rubbed effect" varnish.

We do not claim that this finish is the method used by the old chest painters, but we do feel it is worth while to protect the painted decoration, and this is an excellent way to do it.

CHAPTER XI

Supplies Needed for Painting and Stenciling

Frosted acetate sheeting (also known as Traceolene or Supersee)

Pad of tracing paper (13 x 17 practical size)

Architect's linen (½ yard)

Wax paper — for mounting gold leaf

Conté white pencil

Graphite paper

Lithopone

Stylus pencil

Tack cloth

Masking tape

Pumice stone (FFF)

Rottenstone

Paraffin oil

Carbon tetrachloride

Varnishes: (1) Alcohol-resistant spar or "bar-top" synthetic

           (2) Natural linseed, long-oil varnish. Hard to find. Serviceseal
is an excellent brand, and is available also in black.

Turpentine

Mounted gold leaf

Sandpaper — wet or dry, waterproof garnet or silicon carbide, No. 400–600

Ox-hair varnish brush (used only for varnishing)

Ox-hair "signwriters" brush

Red sable pointed water-color brush, English Size No. 2 best available

Camel-hair quill brushes (small, medium and large)

Striping brushes (large and small with two-inch hairs)

8H drawing pencil (used as a single etcher)

Ivory drop black japan paint for flat black background paint

Red or gray sanding primer

Paints and Other Materials

For the first coat of paint on a tray, use metal sanding primer which comes in gray or red. Apply smoothly by using a soft brush (an ox-hair "signwriters" brush). If it does not spread well, thin it with turpentine. Sanding primer should always be smoothed, when dry, by rubbing with medium waterproof sandpaper and water (paper No. 400). Rinse off and dry tray.

Black backgrounds are made of black japan paint thinned with turpentine to the consistency of thin coffee cream. Japan paint comes in paste form in tubes and in cans. Mix only enough for the surface that is to be covered as it does not keep well. It should be freshly mixed for each coat. This holds true for all japan paints. For colored grounds that have several tints combined to arrive at the exact color, *be sure to strain the paint* just before you apply it. Otherwise particles of each color used may streak the background when the paint is brushed on.

There are several types of varnish used in our painting. Slow-drying varnish is best for stenciling. But do not apply a quick-drying varnish on top of a slow-drying varnish, for in time it will crackle. Alcohol-resistant varnish should be used for finishing trays.

Always use the best artist's oil colors in tubes for painting your patterns. For your work, the following colors are needed: alizarin crimson, chrome yellow medium, Prussian blue, viridian, burnt umber, raw umber, vermilion, permalba white and ivory black. In addition, you may also use: chrome green medium, brown pink, burnt sienna, yellow ochre, raw sienna, Venetian red, mauve, permanent or ultramarine blue, gamboge and Indian yellow.

Enamel undercoat is used as a basic paint when mixing your own tints for painting backgrounds in color. It is a flat paint and covers well. Tints may be made by adding enough tube oil color to give the desired shade or tint. Enamel undercoat is also used when making an underpainting for flowers. It is excellent for striping in white. White oil color is too thin and semi-transparent for striping.

Transparent colors are used for glazes or "floating colors." Among them are the lake colors, and Prussian blue, gamboge, brown pink, viridian and alizarin crimson. Opaque colors have the characteristic of covering the background. Some of them are: white, chrome yellow, chrome green, vermilion, the cadmiums (red and yellow) and the earth colors such as yellow ochre, Venetian red and Indian red.

The finest texture of gold powder is to be found in the lining powders. The finer the texture, the better your finished work will be. The colors needed will be: light or pale gold (lemon), regular gold, antique gold, copper, silver, antique silver and fire-red bronze. There are many shades on the market, but do select the softer colors and avoid the harsh, garish ones.

We use both quill brushes and artist's sable brushes when painting flowers. The same brushes are used when applying gold size for scroll borders. A fine pointed sable brush No. 2 or No. 3 will be the best all-round brush. However, square-tipped quill brushes are excellent for painting large petals on flowers and also for blending colors on flowers and leaves. There is a tendency to use paint that is too thick. Quill brushes are so soft that they do not spread thick paint successfully, and therefore force the painter to thin the paint to the proper consistency. Again we say, several thin coats of paint are better than one thick coat. After using your quills and sable brushes, clean them well in mineral spirits and then saturate the brushes with paraffin oil. We carry our brushes in a flat covered cardboard box. The brushes are held in place with elastic that has been woven through holes in the bottom of the box to form loops for the handles of the brushes. The box is long enough so that the bristles do not touch the end of the box.

Paraffin oil is inexpensive and may be bought from your art supply store. We use it for keeping our brushes soft and for rubbing down trays with pumice stone. We use paraffin oil on *quills and sable brushes only.*

Carbon tetrachloride is used to clean off smudges on your trays. It is a quick cleaner, and must be used at once. Do not allow it to soak into the finish on your tray. It evaporates very quickly and leaves no residue.

Powdered pumice stone should be of the finest texture, at least FFF. Buy it at a drugstore; ask for dental pumice. A bit of powdered pumice and water may be used on a stenciling project (after it has dried) to erase smudges of excess gold powder.

Use an 8H pencil for a single etcher. We find that a single needle etcher is too sharp. The pencil may be sharpened to any point desired. For transferring designs to our tray we use a small ball-point stylus pencil. This saves wear and tear on our patterns. Constant tracing of a pattern with an ordinary pencil will soon obliterate the delicacy of some fine lines and will not make a sharp, clean line on the tray. The stylus pencil leaves no marks on the pattern, and makes a beautiful, sharp line on the tray. Patterns should be fastened to the tray on one side only with Scotch masking tape. This makes it possible to lift the pattern and check the tracing from time to time, making sure that we have not skipped any details. A good tracing is essential. Lithopone, which we use to prepare our tracing paper, is a white opaque paint pigment and comes in powdered form. It is very inexpensive. Lithopone prepared paper is used to transfer the patterns to *dark* backgrounds. Graphite paper is used for *light* backgrounds. This may be bought from your art supply store.

For free-hand sketching of designs on black backgrounds, use a white conté pencil. This is a chalk pencil, and its marks may be easily erased with a damp cloth. We find it superior to silver pencils.

Use pen and ink for making tracings of patterns on your tracing paper. Pencil lines often become smudged and are lost. Pen and ink lines are permanent. Very fine lines may be made with crow quill pens. Use crow quill pens for making fine lines on gold leaf instead of the etching tool, when necessary.

Clean all large brushes with kerosene, except your varnish brush. *Never leave them standing in turpentine.* After cleaning well with kerosene, wash the brushes with yellow laundry soap and warm water. Hang, with bristles down, to dry.

Antiquing Trays

When the design on your tray has been completed, dust the tray well, wipe with a tack cloth and give it a coat of quick-drying varnish. Set it aside in a warm dust-free room to dry. After twenty-four hours rub it *very lightly* with steel wool No. 4/0. Dust well to remove all steel wool particles, then wipe with a tack cloth and give the tray a second coat of varnish. Again wait twenty-four hours; use steel wool as before, dust well and wipe with the tack cloth. Squeeze a bit of brown pink or burnt umber on your palette. Dip your varnish brush into the varnish and varnish the tray quickly. With the tip of the varnish brush pick up some of the brown pink or burnt umber and daub it on the tray in the places where the antiquing is desired. Work the color into the wet varnish until it is well blended and all streaks have disappeared. Better too little antiquing than too much, so be careful! It is always possible to add more antiquing with a subsequent coat of varnish. *Antiquing should not be attempted before the third coat of varnish.* Allow this antiquing coat to dry *forty-eight* hours. Rub *very lightly* with steel wool and give the tray another coat of varnish. At least six coats of bar-top varnish are needed to finish the tray. Each is applied after the tray has been rubbed lightly with steel wool, dusted with a dry cloth, and wiped with a tack cloth.

After the final coat of varnish has dried at least forty-eight hours, use waterproof sandpaper No. 600 and water, to rub down the tray and eliminate every little roughness caused by dust particles. When this has been accomplished, rinse the tray and dry it with a soft cloth.

84

Place the tray flat on a table, sprinkle it with two tablespoonsful of dental pumice stone and add the same amount of paraffin oil. Use a large wad of cotton to rub this mixture over the tray, rubbing back and forth, lengthwise on the tray. Rub lightly as too much pressure may cause scratches. This rubbing process may take an hour or more, as it should be done carefully and thoroughly. Add more dry pumice stone to absorb the oil and gradually wipe off all oil and pumice. Tilt the tray and lightly push this mixture off the tray. When all pumice and oil have been wiped off the tray, polish the tray with a soft clean cotton flannel cloth. Wait three months before waxing the tray with a good quality of paste floor or automobile wax. Waxing the tray helps to prevent scratches.

Do's and Don'ts

1. Never varnish on a cloudy or rainy day.
2. Don't wash sable brushes or quill brushes with water and soap. Wash with turpentine, then use carbon tetrachloride to remove traces of turpentine. Dip in paraffin oil. Allow the oil to remain in these brushes until you are ready to use them again. Then rinse the brushes with turpentine and they are ready to start painting again.

3. Keep your ox-hair varnish brush suspended in turpentine. The bristles must not touch the bottom of the jar. They should clear the bottom by more than an inch. This allows dirt and varnish to settle in the bottom — below the tips of the bristles — and keeps the brush clean. A quart jar is best for this purpose. Cut a hole in the tin cover. Put the handle of the brush through this hole. Place a piece of rubber (taken from an old inner tube) which has had a hole cut in the center of it, over the handle of

For Storing Varnish Brush (suspended in turpentine)

Jar with Excelsior and Mineral Spirits for Washing Sable and Quill Brushes

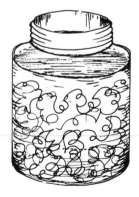

the brush. This holds the brush suspended in the jar of turpentine and also keeps dust out of the jar. The amount of turpentine in the jar is important. It must *completely cover* the bristles of the brush at all times — so that the varnish which is in the brush cannot begin to harden, especially in the heel of the brush. This jar container is illustrated on page 85.

4. For your convenience when painting, keep a pint jar of mineral spirits on your work table for cleaning sable brushes and quill brushes. Place a wad of excelsior in the bottom of this jar. Agitate the brushes against the excelsior to remove the paint. The paint settles to the bottom — leaving clean fluid at the top where you continue to clean your brushes. A diagram is shown on page 85.

5. Just before varnishing or applying a coat of paint, wipe off your tray with a tack cloth to remove all particles of dust.

6. Never let your brush touch the side of the varnish or paint can where there is a chance that it will pick up some of the hardened particles of paint and deposit them on your tray or furniture.

7. It is always better to use several thin coats of paint than one thick coat. This applies to flowers, leaves, etc., as well as backgrounds. On flowers and leaves, pat out the paint with a dry brush or with your finger to keep the paint smooth and thin and to remove all ridges of paint.

8. Don't try to economize by buying inferior grades of brushes. You cannot do fine work with inferior brushes and inferior materials. Ox-hair brushes for varnishing, sable and quill brushes for flower painting, and good quill stripers are necessary for good work.

9. Never use regular or ordinary wax carbon paper for transferring designs to your tray or furniture. Use graphite paper on light backgrounds and lithopone paper on dark grounds. Lithopone paper is prepared by rubbing a small amount of lithopone on a piece of paper taken from your tracing pad. Use a small wad of cotton to distribute the powder. Then use your fingers to rub it well into the pores of the paper and to remove excess loose powder. Fold the paper with lithopone on the inside. Keep it in your tracing pad. It may be used again and again.

Graphite paper may be purchased at your art supply store. If any graphite lines remain on your light backgrounds, they may be erased with art gum.

10. Always wait at least twenty-four hours for each coat of paint or varnish to dry, before applying another coat.

11. Clean brushes that have been used to paint backgrounds in several changes of mineral spirits (substitute for turpentine) or kerosene. Then wash with laundry soap and warm water. Rinse well and hang up to dry.

Either tie a string on the handle to enable you to hang it, or drill a small hole through the handle. It can then be hung on a headless nail. Wash until one hundred per cent clean.

12. Always strain paint through two thicknesses of an old nylon stocking before using on the background of a tray or on furniture. If you are mixing a special color, first do all adding of the tinting color, and all mixing. Then strain the paint last.

13. Use waterproof black sandpaper on trays. Medium fine sandpaper No. 400 or No. 220 with water is used on metal primer paint and No. 600 with water is used on varnished surfaces.

14. Use a conté chalk pencil (white) for sketching free-hand patterns. The chalk is easily eradicated later with a damp cloth.

15. The only use we have for wax paper is for mounting loose gold leaf. *Never use it for anything else in tray work.*

16. Always have bottle caps (with cork and paper removed) to hold a small bit of varnish to be used as a medium while painting with oil colors. Never dip your small brushes into the varnish can.

17. Always keep your can of varnish closed tightly. Keep some small bottles of it in your equipment for use in executing designs so that you will not have to open the can so often. Each time the varnish is exposed to air, it thickens still more. When varnish has become thick, it is no longer good, either for a medium or for finishing coats. Collect small screw top bottles and when you have six or eight, fill them all at one time and seal tightly. Carry one with you to use as your medium when painting.

18. Keep your quill striping brushes in a flat tin box such as a cigarette 50's box. Saturate the brush with paraffin oil and let the oil hold it to the bottom of the box. This helps the brush to stay flat with the hair straight, soft and pliable. When you are ready to use the brush, clean it in the jar of mineral spirits, wipe with a clean dry cloth, and dip it into the striping paint.

19. Varnish trays in a warm room. Never place a freshly varnished tray in a cold room.

20. Patterns in this book have been used many times for trays that come in common sizes. A good way to enlarge or reduce these patterns to fit your special requirement is to bring them to your local blueprint shop.

Photograph 14. Pontypool Decorated Ware

Conclusion

Lace-edge trays, the earliest trays, came in three shapes, round, oval, rectangular — with a perforated rim which gave it the name "Lace-edge." They were decorated with flower sprays, birds, fruits and classical urns.

Chippendale trays were also called "Gothic" and "Pie-crust," while those with flattened rims were known as "Sandwich" rim trays. This Sandwich rim is also found on some old rectangular trays. Their designs were usually fine and elaborate with penned lines or gold scrolls. Birds, flowers, fountains adorned the centers, often painted on a dusted bronze background. Mother-of-pearl was often used on the later trays.

Rectangular trays with rounded corners were produced in all sizes, with and without handle holes. Some of the old ones had Sandwich edges and were decorated with fine "feathery" sprays of gold. Scenes were placed in the centers, including interiors of buildings, landscapes, boating scenes and occasional figures. In fact, all types of decorations were executed on these early trays.

The octagonal "Cut-corner" or "Coffin-lid" tray was an eight-sided tray with a slanting rim. These trays were decorated with simple country designs for the plain country-made trays while the larger and better trays had finer designs of elaborated gold borders both on the rim and floor. The later trays often employed stenciling in their borders, combined with hand-painted leaf sprays.

Oval trays, popular during the nineteenth century, were decorated with many varied designs. Oval trays with a gently curved rim were known as "Windsor" trays.

In some sections of this country antique Chippendale trays in good condition are much sought after and therefore expensive. It is not possible to quote exact prices as the value depends on the period of the tray, its state of preservation, and on the beauty and perfection of the decoration. The rectangular tray seems to be the most common, and consequently may be bought for less. The Gallery trays, Chippendales and Lace-edge have the most value. Miniature trays are scarce and therefore fetch a high price.

Restoring old trays is a fascinating pastime. Study the design and reproduce it in the same way it was done originally. If there is no record of the design, choose one from a similar piece. It would not be good judgment to use a simple country design on a sophisticated piece of tin, or vice-versa. Study your tray, choose the pattern which is of the same period and type, and enjoy the fruits of your labor, knowing that you have restored a lovely old antique.

There is a great satisfaction in this decorative craft for all who like to create beautiful things with their hands. From this fascinating hobby we learn more about color and design, increasing our enjoyment in all hand crafts. It is amazing to discover our capabilities when once we have become absorbed in our painting hobby. There are so many ways of expressing a love of color in our homes, either in wall and furniture decorations, or just in small accessory pieces. A great personal enjoyment is your reward, for you will have pleasure in the anticipation and planning of your decorations as well as pride in the finished product which expresses your own personal touch.